Algorithms Made Simple

Understanding the Building Blocks of Software

WILLIAM E. CLARK

Contents

Preface

In the ever-evolving field of computer science, understanding algorithms is crucial for software development and computational problem-solving. This book, *Algorithms Made Simple: Understanding the Building Blocks of Software*, is crafted to provide readers with a comprehensive foundation in algorithmic theory and practice.

The structure of the book is designed to methodically guide readers from basic programming concepts to complex algorithmic applications. It begins with an introduction to essential programming principles, moving through fundamental data structures, and exploring diverse algorithm design techniques. Core chapters delve into algorithm complexity, analysis, and optimization, equipping the reader with the knowledge to evaluate and improve algorithmic efficiency.

Intended for students, educators, and professionals in computer science, this book balances theoretical insights with practical exercises. Through clear explanations and structured progression, readers will acquire the skills necessary to design, implement, and refine algorithms effectively.

By engaging with the material within these pages, readers can expect

1

to gain a deep understanding of key algorithmic concepts and practical implementation techniques. The book also emphasizes the broader significance of algorithms in various real-world scenarios, encouraging the application of learned skills and fostering a solid foundation for future technological endeavors.

1

Introduction to Programming Concepts

This chapter introduces the fundamental concepts of programming, emphasizing its significance in the creation of software and applications. Readers will learn essential programming terminology and the basic syntax used across various programming languages. The chapter guides beginners through writing their first simple algorithm, showcasing the process of translating ideas into code. Additionally, it introduces pseudocode as a tool for planning algorithms in a structured way. Common errors and debugging techniques are also discussed, equipping readers with the skills to identify and resolve issues in their code.

1.1 What is Programming?

Programming is the process of designing, writing, testing, and maintaining code to create software solutions. At its core, programming involves the transformation of abstract ideas into a structured set of instructions that a computer can execute. This process is highly systematic, combining analytical thinking with a rigorous methodology to develop applications, systems, and utilities that drive modern technology. In its essence, it is about solving problems through the application of logical reasoning and systematic planning.

The significance of programming is evident in its pervasive impact on technological innovation and the operational fabric of many industries. Programming underpins the development of everything from basic applications to complex systems in sectors such as healthcare, finance, transportation, and entertainment. By automating tasks and streamlining processes, programming enables efficiency and scalability, allowing industries to innovate in ways that were previously unimaginable. Additionally, programming is a primary driver of automation, where repetitive tasks are encoded into software to reduce human error and optimize resource utilization.

An essential aspect of learning to program is familiarizing oneself with basic programming terminology. Fundamental terms such as *algorithms, syntax, semantics, variables,* and *functions* lay the groundwork for understanding how programs operate. An algorithm can be defined as a step-by-step procedure for solving a problem or accomplishing a task. Syntax refers to the rules that govern the structure of code, ensuring that the instructions are formed in a way that the computer can interpret. Semantics involves the meaning behind those syntactical el-

4

ements, clarifying what operations the code performs. Variables serve as storage units within a program, holding data values that may change during the execution of a program. Functions, or procedures, allow for the encapsulation of repetitive code blocks, promoting both reusability and modular design.

Central to the field of programming is the programming process itself. This workflow comprises planning, coding, testing, and debugging, each serving a critical role in the development cycle. During the planning stage, developers clearly define the problem and formulate a solution strategy. This is followed by the coding phase, where the solution is implemented in a specific programming language. Testing is then conducted to ensure that the code behaves as expected, and debugging is employed to identify and correct any errors that may arise. This structured approach allows developers to iteratively refine their solutions, gradually building more efficient and robust software.

One of the remarkable aspects of programming is the ability to translate abstract ideas and problem statements into structured, executable code. This translation involves breaking down complex issues into manageable components, each of which can be addressed algorithmically. By methodically analyzing the problem, developers create algorithms that follow a logical progression from problem identification to the final output. Every piece of code, regardless of its complexity, begins as a conceptual idea that is meticulously crafted into a set of detailed instructions.

Programming languages provide the medium through which these instructions are communicated to the computer. A variety of languages exist, each with its own syntax, semantics, and typical application domains. For example, languages such as C and C++ are often used for system programming and performance-critical applications, while languages like Python and JavaScript are favored for rapid development and web-based applications. Each language caters to different programming paradigms and problem domains, making the choice of language an important consideration during the development process.

A classic example that illustrates the essence of programming is the simple 'Hello World' program. This basic program is often the first piece of code written when learning a new programming language, as it demonstrates the most fundamental concept of producing output. The 'Hello World' program is minimal yet significant; it verifies that the programming environment is set up correctly and that the process of writing, compiling (if necessary), and running code is understood. The following is an example of a 'Hello World' program written in a beginner-friendly language:

```
#include <stdio.h>

int main() {
    printf("Hello World\n");
    return 0;
}
```

Beyond the introductory example, it is important to understand the variety of programming paradigms that exist. Different paradigms offer distinct ways to approach coding tasks. Procedural programming, for instance, emphasizes a sequence of steps to achieve a goal, often utilizing functions to encapsulate repetitive tasks. Object-oriented programming, on the other hand, revolves around the concept of objects—data structures that combine attributes and behaviors—and is widely used in large-scale software development. Functional programming, which treats computation as the evaluation of mathematical functions, emphasizes immutability and stateless operations. A comparative understanding of these paradigms allows programmers to select and apply the most appropriate methodology based on the problem at hand.

Equally critical to developing effective programming skills is an understanding of basic syntax elements that form the backbone of any programming language. Syntax encompasses data types, operators, and control structures. Data types define the kinds of values that can be processed, such as integers, floats, strings, and booleans. Operators enable computations and include arithmetic, relational, and logical varieties. Control structures, including conditionals and loops, direct the flow of a program by making decisions and repeating tasks as necessary. Mastery of these elements is crucial as they enable the creation of complex logic from simple building blocks.

In addition to direct coding, planning techniques such as pseudocode are an invaluable skill for programmers. Pseudocode is a high-level description of an algorithm that uses the conventions of programming, but is intended for human reading rather than for execution by a computer. It allows developers to outline the logical flow of a program without being concerned with the specific syntactical detail required by actual programming languages. For example, a pseudocode outline for a simple algorithm might look like this:

```
START
    SET total to 0
    FOR each number in the list
        ADD number to total
    END FOR
    PRINT total
END
```

This form of representation is particularly useful for beginners as it emphasizes logical structuring and sequence without the complications of language-specific syntax. Pseudocode serves as a bridge between the conceptual planning phase and the actual coding phase of software development, offering clarity and coherence in the thought process.

Errors are an inevitable part of programming, especially during the early stages of learning. Common errors typically fall into three primary categories: syntax errors, runtime errors, and logic errors. Syntax errors occur when the code violates the grammatical rules of the programming language, such as missing punctuation or incorrect command structure. Runtime errors arise when the code attempts an invalid operation during execution, such as dividing by zero or accessing unavailable memory. Logic errors, though the most subtle, occur when the code executes without crashing but produces an incorrect result. Awareness of these error types and understanding their mitigation strategies through careful debugging is crucial for developing efficient and error-free code.

Central to mastering programming is a clear grasp of how ideas and algorithms translate into code. Developers must learn to express abstract thoughts—whether it be a mathematical concept, a business requirement, or a user interaction—into a series of logical instructions that guide the computer. This process is integral to bridging the gap between problem analysis and software implementation. By repeatedly practicing this translation, beginners gradually develop an intuition for which programming constructs and language features best capture the desired operations.

Understanding and adopting multiple programming paradigms also enriches a learner's toolkit, allowing for flexible and innovative approaches. For instance, while a procedural approach may be straightforward for small, simple tasks, object-oriented design becomes more effective as the codebase grows in complexity, promoting reusability and better organization. Similarly, functional programming can significantly reduce side effects and make concurrent programming safer and more manageable. The exploration of these paradigms helps in choosing the right techniques that balance clarity, efficiency, and maintainability.

Given the deep interconnection between syntax, semantics, and the logical structure of code, the foundation for becoming proficient in programming is built one small, comprehensible element at a time. From declaring variables to defining functions and mastering control structures, every concept works in concert to create a holistic understanding of how complex applications are formed. Each new concept builds upon previous knowledge, reinforcing the idea that programming is not only about writing code but also about developing a mindset that can dissect, analyze, and address challenging problems systematically.

Working through practical examples and exercises is fundamental in consolidating these concepts. Beginners are encouraged to experiment with small programs, analyze their outputs, and iteratively refine their approaches. In doing so, learners gain firsthand experience in debugging and optimizing their code. This iterative cycle of experimentation, feedback, and improvement is at the heart of the programming process and is key to long-term success in the field.

The basic principles and components covered in this discussion lay the groundwork for more advanced topics. By understanding the process of programming—from conceptualization to execution—readers can better navigate the intricacies of different programming languages and paradigms. The journey from writing a simple "Hello World" program to designing complex software solutions begins with this foundational understanding, which reinforces the crucial link between theoretical principles and practical application.

This section emphasizes that having a strong grip on the basic elements of programming is essential for anyone aspiring to enter the field of software development. Every sophisticated program starts with a well-defined idea, a clear algorithm, and an understanding of the language constructs that bring the idea to life. The challenges encountered in debugging and resolving common errors contribute significantly to a programmer's learning curve, enhancing analytical capabilities and problem-solving skills over time.

The interplay between precise language-specific syntax and the abstract planning achieved through pseudocode also prepares students to approach programming strategically. As the journey continues, these foundational skills will be continually built upon, ultimately enabling the creation of robust and efficient software. The intricate connection between a well-conceived plan and its implementation into code stands as a testament to the intellectual rigor that programming embodies.

1.2 Basic Syntax and Constructs

Programming languages are governed by a set of rules that dictate how various instructions must be written, arranged, and executed. These rules are collectively referred to as syntax, and adherence to them is critical for writing correct code. Syntax establishes the structure of the instructions, ensuring that the computer understands each command as it is intended. If code deviates from these prescribed rules, a compiler or interpreter will typically generate errors, thereby preventing the program from running correctly. Mastery of syntax is foundational because it allows programmers to express their ideas with precision and clarity while translating abstract concepts into concrete operations.

Among the essential elements of programming are data types, which define the kind of data that can be stored and manipulated within a program. Core data types include integers, used for whole numbers; floats, which represent numbers with fractional components; strings, which are sequences of characters used for textual data; and booleans, which express true or false values. Each data type plays a distinct role in how information is handled and processed. For example, integers and floats are typically involved in arithmetic computations, while strings are essential for managing and displaying textual information. The careful use of data types ensures that operations are carried out efficiently and that data is stored in a manner that best suits its intended purpose.

Variables and constants are fundamental constructs in programming that are used for data storage. Variables are mutable entities whose values can change over time, whereas constants are fixed and remain unchanged once they have been declared. The distinction between these two is crucial because it governs how data is maintained throughout the execution of a program. Variables allow the dynamic aspect of programming, adapting to new inputs or changing conditions during runtime. In contrast, constants are used when a fixed value is required, thereby preserving the integrity of data that should not be altered under any circumstances. By using both variables and constants appropriately, code becomes more reliable and easier to maintain.

In addition to data storage, the flow of execution in a program is directed by control structures. These structures enable programmers to dictate the logical sequence of operations based on conditional statements and loops. Conditional statements, such as the if-else construct, allow the program to execute certain blocks of code depending on whether a specific condition is met. For instance, when a condition

11

evaluates to true, the corresponding block is executed; otherwise, an alternative block may be run. As an example, consider the following code snippet that demonstrates the use of an if-else statement:

```
#include <stdio.h>

int main() {
    int number = 10;
    if (number > 0) {
        printf("The number is positive.\n");
    } else {
        printf("The number is non-positive.\n");
    }
    return 0;
}
```

This example shows how a simple conditional construct is used to de-termine which message to display based on the value of the variable number. Control structures extend beyond conditionals to include sev-eral kinds of loops, which are indispensable when a particular task needs to be repeated multiple times. Loops, such as for loops, while loops, and do-while loops, facilitate this repetitive execution. Each loop type provides a different approach to iteration, allowing program-mers to select the most appropriate mechanism based on the specific requirements of the task.

The for loop is one of the most commonly used constructs for iterating over a collection of items or executing a block of code a fixed number of times. It is characterized by having an initialization, a condition, and an increment or update statement all in one concise line. A typical example of a for loop in C is presented below:

```
#include <stdio.h>

int main() {
    int i;
    for (i = 0; i < 5; i++) {
```

```
        printf("Iteration %d\n", i);
    }
    return 0;
}
```

The above snippet demonstrates the iterative process by initializing
a counter, checking a condition at each iteration, and updating the
counter accordingly. This loop continues until the stopping condition
is no longer met, at which point the program exits the loop.

Beyond flow control structures such as conditionals and loops, functions and procedures hold significant importance in programming.
Functions are blocks of code designed to perform specific tasks and can
be easily reused throughout a program. They allow for modularity,
which means that large, complex programs can be decomposed into
smaller, manageable, and reusable components. Declaring functions
typically involves specifying a return type, the function name, and any
parameters that the function requires. The process of calling or invoking these functions within a program not only makes the code more
organized but also enhances readability and maintainability. Here is
a simple example that demonstrates how to declare and invoke a function in a beginner-friendly language:

```
#include <stdio.h>

void greet() {
    printf("Hello! Welcome to programming.\n");
}

int main() {
    greet();
    return 0;
}
```

This function, greet, encapsulates a message that is displayed when

13

the function is called in the main program. The ability to define functions in this way permits code reusability and makes it easier to manage large codebases by reducing repetition and encapsulating functionality.

An integral aspect of writing clear and maintainable code is the inclusion of comments. Comments are non-executable portions of the code that serve to explain and annotate the programmer's intentions. By adding descriptive comments, developers can make their code more comprehensible not only to others who may review or modify it later but also to their future selves when revisiting a project after a significant time lapse. Comments come in various forms depending on the language—single-line comments or multi-line comments are standard features that help demarcate and document critical sections of code.

Basic input and output operations are also central to many programming tasks, particularly those involving interactive applications. Input and output (I/O) operations allow the program to communicate with users by capturing input and displaying results. Simple I/O operations may involve reading a value from the user via a keyboard and printing outputs to the screen. In many programming languages, built-in functions are provided to streamline the process of acquiring and presenting data. For instance, in C, the `scanf` function is used to capture input, and the `printf` function is used to display outputs. This interactive mechanism fosters engagement and makes it easier to verify that a program performs as expected.

Understanding how to identify and resolve syntax errors is a critical skill for any programmer. Syntax errors are the result of incorrect code that violates a language's formal specifications, and they prevent the program from compiling or running correctly. Common syntax errors include missing semicolons, unmatched parentheses, or improper nesting of control structures. Basic debugging techniques often involve reading error messages carefully, checking the corresponding code line, and methodically examining the sequence of instructions to ensure that all syntactical rules are followed correctly. Debugging is not only a valuable skill in correcting errors but also a significant part of learning to write reliable and efficient code.

Throughout the process of learning programming, understanding the interplay of these fundamental concepts is imperative. Syntax provides the framework within which every other component exists—ensuring that data types are declared correctly, variables are accurately manipulated, and control structures operate as intended. Data types, variables, and constants work in tandem to store and manage data, enabling programs to perform computations and respond to user inputs. Control structures, including conditionals and loops, dictate the flow of execution and support the dynamic nature of real-world applications. Functions and procedures encapsulate reusable code segments, making programs more organized and modular. By integrating comments and utilizing effective debugging practices, programmers can maintain clarity and innovation throughout their code development process.

Learning these basic constructs lays a solid foundation for tackling more advanced programming challenges. When beginners invest time in mastering syntax and understanding how basic control structures and data types interact, they develop the critical skills required to transition from writing simple scripts to creating complex, scalable software systems. It is through the rigorous application of these fundamentals that programmers can confidently structure their code, anticipate potential errors, and refine their approaches to solving problems more efficiently.

Each concept described here relates directly to the day-to-day duties of coding and software development. The discipline required to write syntactically correct code, along with the ability to employ conditional logic, iterate over data, and modularize via functions, cannot be understated. With practice, the awareness of correct syntax becomes second nature, much like the fluency of a native language. This fluency allows a programmer to focus on solving higher-level problems rather than becoming bogged down by low-level errors.

The building blocks of programming that are discussed form an interdependent framework. For example, the proper use of data types avoids type mismatches that could lead to runtime errors, while structured control flows maintain logical consistency. Likewise, the use of comments not only documents the code's purpose but also acts as an invaluable resource during debugging sessions. By adhering to these principles, a programmer can design programs that are both efficient and effective, mitigating issues before they escalate into formidable obstacles.

Ultimately, the foundation built upon understanding syntax, data types, variables, control structures, and functions is critical for any aspiring developer. This grasp of basic syntax and constructs empowers programmers to write clearer and more efficient code—a necessary step in the journey towards mastering complex programming paradigms and techniques. The practices that are instilled during this phase of learning pave the way for future success in more advanced courses and real-world software development scenarios. With a constant focus on clarity, precision, and correctness, the journey of programming becomes a well-organized progression from simple code snippets to comprehensive, full-scale software solutions.

1.3   Writing Your First Algorithm

An algorithm is a finite set of clear instructions designed to perform a specific task or to solve a problem. It forms the backbone of all computational processes and represents a systematic approach to processing data and reaching conclusions. In programming, an algorithm is not merely a theoretical concept; it is the bridge between problem-solving and coding, serving as the roadmap that guides every line of code toward achieving a desired outcome.

When embarking on the task of writing your first algorithm, it is advisable to start with a simple and manageable problem. A commonly suggested exercise for beginners is to design an algorithm that sums a list of numbers. This problem is elementary but encapsulates several fundamental techniques: handling input, processing data sequentially, and producing output. Breaking the problem down into these basic steps allows for a gradual learning curve while demonstrating the real-world application of logical thinking in code development.

The first step in writing an algorithm is to understand the problem completely. This involves reading the problem statement carefully and determining what data is required, what operations need to be performed, and what the expected result should be. For the problem of summing a list of numbers, the input is a collection of numerical values; the process involves iterating through the list and adding each number to a running total; and the output is the final sum. Clarifying these components at the onset provides a focused goal and serves as a guide for structuring both the pseudocode and the actual program.

A recommended practice during the planning stage is to start with pseudocode. Pseudocode is a plain language description that outlines

17

the logical steps of the algorithm without the precise syntax of any specific programming language. This abstraction helps in organizing thoughts and ensures that the underlying logic is sound before translating it into executable code. For instance, the pseudocode for a summing algorithm can be structured as follows:

```
START
    SET total to 0
    GET list of numbers
    FOR each number in the list
        ADD number to total
    END FOR
    OUTPUT total
END
```

This pseudocode effectively communicates the algorithm's flow: initializing a total variable, iterating through each element in a list, and producing the sum. It places an emphasis on the structure and logic without bogging down in the technicalities of a specific language's syntax.

Following the creation of pseudocode, the next phase is translating this logical structure into a complete, executable program. Translating pseudocode into code involves selecting an appropriate programming language and mapping each step of the pseudocode to its corresponding syntactical construct. For beginners, a language like C is often recommended due to its straightforward syntax and widespread use in educational contexts. Let us consider a complete code implementation in C for the summing algorithm:

```
#include <stdio.h>

int main() {
    int n, i;
    int sum = 0;
    printf("Enter the number of elements: ");
```

```
scanf("%d", &n);
int numbers[n];

printf("Enter %d numbers:\n", n);
for(i = 0; i < n; i++) {
    scanf("%d", &numbers[i]);
}

for(i = 0; i < n; i++) {
    sum += numbers[i];
}

printf("The total sum is: %d\n", sum);
return 0;
}
```

This code begins by including a standard input-output header, followed by the declaration of the main function along with necessary variables. The program prompts the user to input the number of elements in the list, and then it reads each number into an array. A second loop traverses the array to accumulate the sum. Finally, the program prints the total sum to the console. Such a step-by-step translation ensures that the foundational logic from pseudocode is faithfully recreated in code, thus reinforcing the understanding of programming constructs.

Executing an algorithm involves compiling the code and running the resultant program. When you compile your code, the compiler translates the high-level instructions into machine code, and any syntax errors or issues are flagged during this process. For the simple summing algorithm, after compilation, you can execute the program from a command-line interface. When prompted, you may enter a series of numbers, and then the program computes and displays their sum. An example of how a program execution might appear is given below:

```
Enter the number of elements: 5
```

```
Enter 5 numbers:
10
20
30
40
50
The total sum is: 150
```

This output demonstrates that the program successfully processes the user inputs and generates the correct result by adhering to the steps outlined in the algorithm.

Testing the algorithm is a crucial part of the development process. It involves running the program with a wide range of inputs to verify that it behaves as expected under various conditions. For instance, you might test the summing algorithm with different sizes of the input list, including edge cases such as an empty list or a list containing negative numbers. Testing not only confirms that the algorithm is correct, but it also helps to identify any hidden logical errors or inefficiencies that might not be evident during a single run.

Addressing common coding issues is also an integral skill for beginners. During the translation of pseudocode to code, issues such as off-by-one errors in loops, improper handling of user inputs, and misconceptions about variable initialization can arise. Systematic testing and debugging are key strategies in identifying and resolving these problems. Techniques such as using print statements to check variable values, stepping through code with a debugger, or even conducting peer reviews are effective ways to troubleshoot and ensure the program is working precisely as intended.

Beyond simply making your code run, it is important to iteratively improve the algorithm. Iteration in algorithm design means revisiting the initial solution and optimizing it or expanding its functionality.

Once the basic summing algorithm is functional, you might consider enhancements such as adding error checking to manage invalid input or modifying the program to handle floating-point numbers in addition to integers. Continuous refinement not only improves the robustness of the program but also deepens one's understanding of both the problem domain and the programming language used.

In addition to the learning process of writing one's first algorithm, it is essential to appreciate that algorithms are foundational to all higher-level programming and data processing tasks. Every sophisticated software solution, no matter how complex, is built upon simple concepts that have been iteratively refined over time. By mastering a simple task like summing a list of numbers, beginners build confidence and acquire the analytical skills required for tackling more advanced algorithms in the future.

The journey from conceptualizing a problem to executing an algorithm involves several distinct yet interconnected stages. Initially, one must choose a problem that is not overwhelming in complexity yet allows room to learn fundamental programming capabilities. Understanding the problem and breaking it down into manageable steps solidifies the ability to design algorithms logically. Following this, converting these logical steps into pseudocode creates a bridge between abstract reasoning and practical coding. Translating pseudocode into an actual programming language then solidifies this bridge, providing a working example that demonstrates every aspect of the algorithm from input handling to output generation.

An emphasis on the systematic structure of algorithms—starting with high-level planning in pseudocode, moving through systematic code creation, and culminating in rigorous testing—reaffirms the importance of planning and problem decomposition. Every successful execu-

21

tion of a program is rooted in clear logic and an understanding of how data is processed and manipulated through code. This methodology forms the basis of computer programming and is echoed throughout all levels of software development.

Furthermore, this approach reflects a broader principle central to problem-solving in computing: start simple and iterate. The initial summing algorithm serves as an entry point. It demonstrates that even the simplest problems require thorough logical structuring. As learners become more comfortable, they are encouraged to experiment with additional features, modify control structures, and incorporate advanced data handling techniques. Over time, these iterative improvements cultivate a mindset geared towards continuous improvement—a quality that is indispensable in the ever-evolving field of technology.

Recognizing common coding issues is integral to refining initial attempts at algorithm construction. It is normal to encounter obstacles in the debugging phase, yet each error resolved contributes to practical knowledge and expertise. The errors encountered during the development process provide insights into both the limitations of programming environments and the intricacies of logical thought. Approaching these issues with persistence and attention to detail helps to transform obstacles into learning milestones.

In essence, a successful algorithm is one that not only produces the correct output but is also transparent, maintainable, and adaptable to changes. The practice of writing and then gradually improving an algorithm is reflective of the broader iterative nature of software development. With each iteration, the algorithm becomes more refined, and the programmer gains a deeper understanding of both the problem and the solution methods available.

Engaging with algorithm development through a structured process—from conceptualization through execution—prepares learners for more complex challenges. Whether used to automate mundane tasks or solve intricate problems, the algorithmic approach remains a fundamental skill for any aspiring programmer. The insights gained from writing a simple summing algorithm thus serve as stepping stones toward more ambitious projects, where the same principles of planning, coding, testing, and optimization apply, albeit on a larger and more complex scale.

By embracing the concept of algorithms and the discipline required to write them, beginners lay down a robust foundation for their journey in programming. Each element—from the initial problem selection to the final improvements in the code—cultivates an environment where systematic problem-solving replaces guesswork and uncertainty. In this manner, the process of writing and executing a simple algorithm evolves into a comprehensive learning experience, imparting essential techniques that will be applicable across various programming challenges throughout one's career.

1.4   Pseudocode

Pseudocode is a streamlined, language-agnostic method for expressing the logic of an algorithm. It serves as an intermediary representation that bridges the gap between human reasoning and programming language syntax. Pseudocode allows individuals to articulate the steps and control flows of an algorithm without being confined to the strict rules of specific programming languages. By doing so, it simplifies the planning phase of algorithm development, enabling the focus to remain on clear logical structure and problem-solving techniques.

The primary purpose of pseudocode is to facilitate the planning and design of algorithms. When writing pseudocode, one is not burdened by intricate syntax details; instead, the emphasis is placed on conveying ideas and the flow of logic. This clarity of intention helps programmers and algorithm designers communicate their approach succinctly. Pseudocode is particularly useful during brainstorming and initial problem analysis, as it allows for rapid iteration over ideas and adjustments in the algorithm's structure before investing time in writing and debugging actual code.

At its core, the basic structure of pseudocode is quite minimalistic and easy to grasp. A well-constructed pseudocode script typically includes clear definitions of control statements such as conditionals and loops, logical separators like indentation, and explicit notations for operations. For instance, pseudocode utilizes keywords like IF, ELSE, FOR, WHILE, and RETURN to articulate decisions, repetitions, and termination of tasks. Indentation is used to denote blocks of logic, mirroring the structure seen in many high-level programming languages. This structure not only aids in clarity but also in maintaining an organized overview of the algorithm's flow.

Common pseudocode conventions have evolved to standardize the representation of programming concepts. While pseudocode does not require strict adherence to one particular style, there are widely accepted practices that help maintain clarity and consistency. For example:

- IF and ELSE are commonly employed to denote decision-making points.

- FOR and WHILE are used to indicate iterative processes.

- Keywords such as BEGIN, END, or simple indentation help encapsulate blocks of code.

- RETURN is often used to indicate the conclusion of a function or the output of an algorithm.

Maintaining consistency in these conventions ensures that anyone reading the pseudocode can easily follow the intended logic without needing to decipher unconventional syntax.

The process of writing an algorithm in pseudocode begins with a clear understanding of the problem to be solved. It is essential to break down the problem into manageable components and then outline the logical steps required to address each part of the problem. For instance, if the task is to design an algorithm to sort a list of numbers, the pseudocode should clearly state how the list will be traversed, what comparisons will be made, and how the elements will be rearranged. Drafting these steps in pseudocode serves as a blueprint for the subsequent coding process.

To illustrate this process, consider a simple problem: finding the largest number in a list. The following pseudocode outlines how one might approach this problem:

```
BEGIN
    SET max to first element of list
    FOR each element in the list starting from second element
        IF current element > max THEN
            SET max to current element
        END IF
    END FOR
    OUTPUT max
END
```

This example clearly demonstrates the structure of a straightforward algorithm. The pseudocode begins with an initialization step, sets up a loop to iterate through the elements, uses a conditional structure to compare values, and finally outputs the result. Such examples help in understanding how high-level logic is broken down into an easily digestible format which can then be translated into actual code.

One of the significant advantages of pseudocode is the ease with which it can be compared to actual code. In many cases, when developers move from pseudocode to an implemented program, they find that the pseudocode serves as a detailed guide that ensures every logical step is accounted for. Whereas actual code requires strict syntax, pseudocode can focus on the reasoning behind each operation. This comparison highlights the planning advantages: pseudocode remains concise and clear, avoiding the verbosity and potential for distraction inherent in full programming language syntax.

Translating pseudocode to actual code is a vital step in the development process. Once the logic has been clearly defined and understood through pseudocode, a programmer is in a strong position to convert the abstract steps into a specific programming language. This translation requires mapping each pseudocode construct to its corresponding code construct. For example, an IF statement in pseudocode will typically be translated to an if...else statement in languages like C, Java, or Python. A FOR loop in pseudocode will become a loop construct in the chosen language, complete with initialization, condition-checking, and incrementation. Care must be taken during this translation to ensure that the original logic remains intact and that any nuances in language syntax are properly handled.

Despite its simplicity, writing pseudocode is not without pitfalls. Common mistakes in pseudocode include overcomplicating the logic with unnecessary details, which can detract from the overall clarity, or conversely, omitting critical steps leading to ambiguous instructions. Beginners may also struggle with appropriate use of indentation or misapplying common keywords, leading to confusion when transitioning to actual code. To avoid these issues, it is advised that one focuses on clear, concise language and maintains uniformity in the use of conventions. Reviewing pseudocode with peers or mentors and comparing it to established examples can provide additional guidance and help in refining the approach.

Using pseudocode for planning is a strategy that should be incorporated early in the problem-solving process. By writing pseudocode before embarking on the coding phase, developers can map out their thinking in a structured manner, identify potential logical flaws, and make modifications without the overhead of recompilation or debugging. This proactive approach not only smooths the development process but also enhances one's ability to communicate complex ideas to others. In team environments, pseudocode serves as a common language that can bridge varying levels of technical expertise and ensures that all team members are aligned on the intended functionality of the application.

To further engage in effective pseudocode practice, consider adopting a simple exercise. Choose an everyday problem, such as calculating the factorial of a number, and write pseudocode for it. Here is an example of how one might approach this exercise:

```
BEGIN
    INPUT number
    SET factorial to 1
    FOR i from 1 to number
        SET factorial to factorial * i
    END FOR
    OUTPUT factorial
```

END

This exercise encourages the writer to focus on logical flow and concise expression of computations. By practicing with such exercises, beginners can gradually build confidence in structuring their thoughts without immediately worrying about the details of any specific programming language.

Pseudocode is also particularly useful in educational settings, where the emphasis is on understanding rather than memorizing syntax. Instructors often use pseudocode to explain complex algorithms in a way that is accessible to beginners. It strips away the language-specific elements and allows learners to focus on the core logic. Furthermore, pseudocode can be instrumental in situations that require rapid prototyping or when a clear presentation of the algorithm's design is necessary for collaborative projects.

Another important benefit of pseudocode is its role in debugging and refining algorithms. When faced with a problem, having a clear pseudocode version can help developers track where errors might be occurring. Instead of scouring through lines of intricate code, one can refer back to the pseudocode to ensure that the intended logic is correctly represented in the actual code. This back-and-forth process between pseudocode and code helps in identifying discrepancies and refining the solution iteratively.

Moreover, pseudocode has a flexible nature that encourages experimentation. Since pseudocode is not bound by strict syntax, developers can quickly sketch out alternative solutions and compare their effectiveness. This flexibility reduces the time spent on trial and error during early stages of problem-solving and increases productivity by allowing multiple approaches to be considered before committing to one particular implementation.

In practice, regularly writing and refining pseudocode fosters a habit of careful planning, which is critical for tackling more complex programming challenges. By beginning with a clear and concise outline of the desired outcome, programmers are better prepared to handle unexpected issues that may arise later in the development cycle. It instills a mindset of thorough analysis and proactive troubleshooting, ultimately leading to the creation of more robust, efficient, and maintainable code.

The process of converting pseudocode into executable code is akin to translation, where the clarity of the original message must be preserved while adapting to the constraints of the target language. This conversion reinforces the importance of precise logical structuring, as any ambiguity in the pseudocode can lead to potential errors in the final program. By ensuring that the pseudocode is detailed, logical, and unambiguous, developers lay a solid foundation for successful programming endeavors.

Pseudocode is an invaluable tool in the realm of algorithm design. It provides a format for expressing the logical structure of an algorithm in a clear and understandable manner. Its purpose is to simplify complex ideas, allowing for a focus on problem-solving without the distraction of syntax errors. Through the use of a basic structure, common conventions, and clear notation, pseudocode acts as a preparatory step that transforms abstract ideas into actionable plans. As a preliminary tool, it facilitates effective planning, clearer communication, and smoother translation into executable code. Beginners are encouraged to integrate pseudocode into their learning process to develop a disciplined approach to algorithm design. By engaging in practice exercises and continuously refining their pseudocode, learners can build a strong foundation that will serve them throughout their programming careers.

1.5   Common Errors and Debugging Tips

Errors in programming occur for a variety of reasons and can significantly impact the execution of code. At their core, errors are deviations from the expected behavior of a program that result from mistakes made during coding or misinterpretations of problem requirements. These deviations can be caused by simple typographical errors, complex logical oversights, or even miscommunications between different parts of a program. Understanding why errors occur and how they affect program execution is crucial for developing robust and reliable software. Errors not only hinder the smooth operation of a program but also serve as indicators of areas that require closer attention and refinement.

Errors in programming are generally categorized into three main types: syntax errors, runtime errors, and logic errors. Syntax errors occur when the code does not conform to the grammatical rules defined by the programming language. These errors are typically detected by the compiler or interpreter, preventing the program from running until they are resolved. Common examples of syntax errors include misspelled keywords, missing punctuation such as semicolons or parentheses, or improper nesting of code blocks. For instance, forgetting to terminate a statement with a semicolon in a language like C often results in a clear syntax error message that points out the line where the issue occurs. Resolving syntax errors usually involves closely reviewing the code for such typographical mistakes and ensuring that each command adheres to the language's syntactical rules.

Runtime errors, on the other hand, occur during the execution of a program. These errors are not detected by the compiler because the code is syntactically correct; rather, they manifest when the program encounters an operation that it cannot perform. Examples of runtime errors include dividing a number by zero, attempting to access an undefined variable or array element, or performing an invalid type conversion. Such errors are often influenced by external factors like user input or system resources. The challenge with runtime errors is that they may only appear under certain conditions or with specific datasets, which makes them harder to predict and diagnose.

Logic errors represent another category of programming errors and are perhaps the most subtle of all. Unlike syntax or runtime errors, logic errors occur when the code runs without interruption but produces an unintended or incorrect output. These errors stem from faulty reasoning or flawed algorithm design. For example, an algorithm intended to calculate the average of a list of numbers might sum the values correctly yet mistakenly divide by an incorrect count, resulting in an inaccurate average. Logic errors can be the most difficult type of error to identify because there may be no explicit indication through error messages. Instead, the programmer must rely on careful analysis of the program's output and behavior to pinpoint where the logical flaw lies.

Given the inevitability of errors, employing effective debugging strategies is essential for any programmer, especially beginners. One of the most practical methods for debugging is to isolate sections of code and execute them step-by-step. This process helps confirm whether each segment behaves as expected before integrating it into the larger pro-

31

gram. Using print statements strategically is an invaluable technique in this regard. By inserting print statements into the code, developers can track variable values and document the flow of execution as the program runs. For example, printing the value of a counter within a loop or outputting intermediate results can help verify that the logic is working correctly at every stage. This method not only aids in understanding the program's behavior but also makes it easier to locate the source of an error.

Understanding and interpreting error messages provided by the programming environment is another crucial step in debugging. Most compilers and interpreters offer detailed error messages that specify the nature of the error, the location in the code where it occurred, and sometimes even suggestions for resolving it. By carefully reading these messages, programmers can rapidly narrow down the area of the code that requires fixing. Over time, as one becomes more familiar with common errors and their associated messages, resolving issues becomes a more intuitive process.

Collaborating with peers through code reviews can also be a powerful strategy for debugging. A fresh pair of eyes may spot errors or inefficiencies that the original author overlooked. Peer review not only enhances the quality of code but also serves as an educational experience, allowing programmers to learn from each other's mistakes and successes. In team environments, engaging in regular code reviews fosters an atmosphere of continual learning and quality assurance, benefiting both the individual programmer and the project as a whole.

It is important for beginners to be aware of some of the common mistakes that are frequently made when writing code. Novice programmers often struggle with issues such as off-by-one errors in loops, misusing variable scopes, neglecting to initialize variables, or misunderstanding control structures. These mistakes can lead to errors that, although sometimes minor, may result in significant deviations from the intended behavior of the program. To prevent such errors, beginners should take care to write code methodically. This involves planning the structure of the program in advance, carefully defining the purpose and scope of each variable, and thoroughly testing each section of the code as it is developed. Adopting a systematic approach to coding reduces the likelihood of errors and builds a stronger foundation for more advanced programming tasks.

Modern integrated development environments (IDEs) come equipped with a range of debugging tools that can significantly streamline the error resolution process. Features such as breakpoints, step-through debugging, and variable watches allow programmers to inspect the state of a program at specific execution points. By pausing the execution of the program at strategic locations, developers can examine the values of variables and understand precisely how the program state evolves. This real-time inspection is especially useful for pinpointing subtle logic errors that might not be apparent through standard testing methods. Utilizing these IDE features, along with traditional techniques like print statements, can dramatically reduce the time and effort required to identify and resolve errors.

In addition to IDE features, leveraging online communities and resources can provide additional support when debugging proves challenging. Many programming forums, discussion boards, and collaborative platforms offer valuable insights, tips, and solutions to common coding issues. For beginners, tapping into these resources not only helps solve immediate problems but also builds a broader understanding of debugging techniques and best practices within the programming community.

While debugging can be a time-consuming process, maintaining a positive mindset and persistent attitude is critical. Every error resolved is an opportunity to deepen one's understanding of programming and to grow as a coder. Embracing errors as a natural part of the learning process, rather than viewing them solely as obstacles, fosters resilience and encourages a methodical approach to problem-solving. Persistence, combined with methodical testing and a willingness to seek assistance, is crucial for overcoming debugging challenges.

Best practices in debugging involve not only resolving current errors but also implementing changes that prevent similar issues in the future. Writing maintainable and well-documented code can significantly reduce the frequency and impact of errors. Structured code with clear comments, logical segmentation, and consistent formatting makes it easier to review and identify inconsistencies. Additionally, incorporating automated testing frameworks into the development workflow can help catch errors as soon as they are introduced, thereby facilitating continuous improvement and reliability in code execution.

The journey of learning to debug is iterative and continual. As programmers gain experience, their ability to anticipate potential errors improves. Furthermore, developing a structured approach to debugging — one that starts with isolating a problem, utilizes logical reasoning, and employs a combination of print statements and IDE tools — can save considerable time during development. Over time, these techniques become second nature, enabling a more fluid and effective coding process.

Even after resolving errors, it is beneficial to reflect on the mistake and understand its root cause. This reflective practice helps in identifying patterns in recurring errors and strengthens one's ability to write error-resistant code in the future. Troubleshooting a complex error once, and then recognizing similar signs in subsequent coding sessions, builds a mental framework for anticipating and mitigating potential issues before they manifest.

Ultimately, the development of strong debugging skills is an essential part of becoming a proficient programmer. It involves a delicate balance between technical knowledge, logical reasoning, and practical application. This section underscores the importance of understanding error types, employing effective debugging strategies, and remaining persistent in the face of challenges. Through continuous practice, proactive learning, and the integration of available resources and tools, programmers can significantly improve the accuracy, reliability, and efficiency of their code.

Maintaining a patient and analytical approach to debugging will not only enhance coding proficiency but also instill a comprehensive understanding of how programs function. As each error is addressed and resolved, the overall quality of the code improves, paving the way for the development of increasingly complex and reliable software solutions. In this journey, every debugging session provides valuable insights, turning obstacles into stepping stones toward mastery of the art of programming.

2

Introduction to Algorithms and Complexity

This chapter delves into the foundational concepts of algorithms, defining them as step-by-step procedures for problem-solving in computing. It explores various fundamental strategies used in algorithm design, such as recursion, iteration, and the divide and conquer approach. The chapter introduces asymptotic analysis, explaining how Big O, Big Theta, and Big Omega notations are utilized to express algorithm performance in relation to input size. Readers will learn to evaluate the efficiency of algorithms by examining their runtime and memory usage. Additionally, the trade-offs between time and space complexity are discussed, providing insight into practical considerations when implementing algorithms.

2.1   Defining Algorithms

Algorithms are defined as precise, step-by-step instructions designed to solve specific problems or perform designated tasks in computing. They provide a systematic procedure that transforms input data into output results by following a clearly defined set of operations. In computing, an algorithm is not merely a sequence of operations; it is a carefully crafted plan that ensures each step is unambiguous and operationally effective. The fundamental idea behind an algorithm is its ability to take an initial input, process that input through a series of determinate steps, and produce an output that meets predetermined criteria.

The importance of algorithms in computing cannot be overstated. They are the backbone of software development and form the core of problem solving in technology. Efficient algorithms can reduce computation time and resource usage dramatically, often determining the feasibility of a complex application. By breaking down complicated tasks into smaller, manageable steps, algorithms empower programmers to build solutions that are robust, scalable, and reliable. In modern computing, innovations such as search engines, data encryption, and artificial intelligence all rely on well-designed algorithms. Algorithms drive advancements in technology by facilitating logical reasoning and efficient processing, making it possible to tackle increasingly challenging problems in various fields.

A well-formed algorithm is characterized by several essential properties which ensure its reliability and effectiveness. First, finiteness is a critical property: an algorithm must have a finite number of steps, guaranteeing that the process will eventually terminate. Definiteness is also a requirement; every instruction in an algorithm must be precisely defined and free from ambiguity. Additionally, clear input and output specifications are necessary, ensuring that an algorithm knows what data it starts with and what it is expected to produce. Effectiveness is another vital characteristic; each step in the algorithm should be sufficiently basic that it can be executed by a human, a machine, or a computational model. Together, these properties create a framework that distinguishes effective, well-formed algorithms from vague or overly complex procedures.

An effective algorithm can be deconstructed into its core components: the initial inputs, the processing steps, and the outputs. The process begins with the input, which represents the data or parameters that the algorithm will work with. This input is then subjected to a sequence of clearly defined operations. Each of these operations transforms the data in some way, gradually moving toward the final solution. Finally, the defined outputs are produced, representing the result of all the computational work done by the algorithm. This structural clarity is what enables algorithms to be implemented consistently in various programming languages and systems, ensuring that the intended operations are performed regardless of the underlying hardware or software environment.

Algorithms serve as systematic procedures for problem solving by providing a logical progression from a known state to a desired result. In any situation where a problem must be resolved—whether it is sorting a dataset, searching for an element, or processing a complex mathematical calculation—algorithms offer a sequence of well-defined steps. They break the problem into smaller, manageable sub-tasks that are easier to solve, using either repetition, conditional branching, or a combination of both. This structured approach not only simplifies complex tasks but also offers a clear roadmap for debugging and future enhancements. As a result, algorithms are essential tools for transforming abstract ideas into programmable solutions.

Everyday examples of algorithms are abundant in both everyday life and computing. Consider the process of sorting a list of names or finding the shortest path in a network. In the case of sorting, an algorithm such as bubble sort or merge sort systematically compares and rearranges items in a list until they are in the desired order. For finding the shortest path, an algorithm like Dijkstra's or A* examines various pathways, discards non-optimal routes, and ultimately identifies the most efficient route from one point to another. Such examples demonstrate how algorithms are inherently practical, providing clear, step-by-step methodologies that have real-world applications.

Visual representations of algorithms can further enhance understanding. One common method is the use of flowcharts, which graphically depict the sequence of operations and decision points within the algorithm. A simplified flowchart can be represented in a table format. For instance, consider the following tabular depiction:

Step	Operation
1	Start the process
2	Receive input data
3	Process the input through predefined operations
4	Evaluate conditions and make decisions
5	Produce output data
6	End the process

Table 2.1: *Flowchart Representation of a Basic Algorithm*

This table illustrates how a flowchart can communicate the procedure in a clear format. Each row in the table corresponds to a distinct step in the process, mapping out the operational flow and decision-making points inherent in the algorithm. Such visual aids are invaluable for beginners as they facilitate comprehension of abstract concepts by breaking down procedural logic into digestible parts.

Bridging the gap between visual representations and actual implementation is the use of pseudocode. Pseudocode provides a simplified, language-agnostic notation that enables one to express the logic of an algorithm in a way that is easily translatable to any programming language. Consider the following example of pseudocode for an algorithm that finds the maximum number in a list:

```
Algorithm FindMaximum(List)
    Input: List of numbers
    Output: Maximum number in the list

    max_value <- List[0]
    for each number in List do
        if number > max_value then
            max_value <- number
        end if
    end for
    return max_value
End Algorithm
```

This pseudocode clearly illustrates the logical steps of the algorithm: initializing a variable, iterating through each element in the list, conditionally updating the maximum value, and finally returning the result. Such representations are valuable for programmers as they provide a clear, language-independent description of the algorithm's logic that can later be implemented in any specific programming language.

Beyond structure and representation, evaluating the effectiveness of an algorithm is an important practice. The performance of an algorithm can be assessed through criteria such as correctness, efficiency, and robustness. Correctness ensures that the algorithm produces the intended output for all valid inputs. Efficiency pertains to how quickly and resourcefully the algorithm performs its tasks, often evaluated in terms of time complexity and space requirements. Robustness is the ability of an algorithm to handle unexpected or extreme input conditions without failure. Using these criteria, one can rigorously test and validate algorithms, ensuring that they are not only functional but also optimized for practical use.

Despite the clarity that algorithms can bring to problem solving, several common pitfalls often hinder their design. One frequent mistake is the creation of ambiguous instructions, where a step in the algorithm is not clearly defined, leading to misinterpretation during implementation. Another error is the oversight of edge cases—situations that occur at the extreme ends of the input spectrum—which can cause an otherwise correct algorithm to fail. Incomplete specifications regarding input and output expectations also contribute to the failure of an algorithm. Recognizing these pitfalls is essential for designing more precise algorithms; careful planning and thorough testing are key strategies to mitigate such errors.

The role of algorithms as fundamental problem-solving procedures is further highlighted through their diverse applications. In scientific computing, algorithms are used to model and simulate complex phenomena. In data analytics, they help in sorting, filtering, and extracting meaningful insights from vast datasets. In everyday computing, tasks such as file searching, data encryption, and network routing all rely on the systematic approach provided by algorithms. This widespread applicability underscores the importance of understanding the intricacies of algorithm design, as a well-crafted algorithm not only solves a problem but also optimizes the use of time and space resources.

When developing algorithms, it is crucial to adhere to structured design principles that promote clarity and efficiency. By breaking down the problem into its basic components—inputs, processing steps, and outputs—programmers can systematically construct solutions that are both scalable and maintainable. Emphasizing precision in every step ensures that algorithms remain unambiguous and effective, an approach that is particularly beneficial when transitioning from pseudocode representations to actual programming code.

Through systematic breakdowns and representations, algorithms embody the essence of logical sequencing and computational problem solving. They not only guide the step-by-step execution of tasks but also empower developers to innovate and optimize software solutions. Whether dealing with simple operations such as arithmetic calculations or complex computations like machine learning models, the principles underlying algorithm design remain consistent. This consistency allows learners to build a solid foundation that supports more advanced topics in computer science and software engineering.

The integration of clear definitions, graphic representations, and structured pseudocode in explaining algorithms provides learners a comprehensive view of how these procedures function in both theoretical and practical contexts. Throughout the study of algorithms, learners encounter various important components—from initial input handling to iterative processing and decision-making—each contributing to a full understanding of systematic problem solving. Recognizing the characteristics of algorithms enables learners to appreciate the rigorous nature of computational procedures, while the numerous real-world examples reinforce the ubiquitous nature of these systems.

Embracing a methodical approach when designing algorithms fosters a mindset that values detailed planning and careful evaluation of each step. Such a mindset is essential for developing solutions that not only resolve the problem at hand but also perform efficiently under varying conditions. By continuously iterating on algorithm design, adjusting for common mistakes, and validating effectiveness through testing, developers lay the groundwork for robust and innovative software solutions.

The comprehensive understanding of what algorithms are, their role in computing, and how they provide logical, step-by-step problem solving is central to the progression of any programmer. Integrating clear definitions, practical illustrations, structured pseudocode, and visual representations equips beginners with the tools necessary to navigate the complexities of modern computing. This foundational knowledge is indispensable for constructing algorithms that are both theoretically sound and practically efficient, thereby driving forward technological innovation and enhancing problem solving across numerous domains.

2.2   Fundamental Strategies

Problem-solving in programming involves applying systematic methods to break down complex challenges into manageable parts. Logical reasoning and structured thinking are essential in formulating effective solutions. Various strategies can be employed to approach programming tasks, each with distinct characteristics and best use cases. Among the most common are recursion, iteration, and divide and conquer techniques. These methods provide different frameworks for addressing problems: recursion offers elegant solutions for tasks with a naturally self-referential structure, iteration provides a straightforward methodology for repeated operations, and divide and conquer splits a complex task into simpler subproblems that are solved independently before combining their outcomes.

Recursion is a powerful technique in which a function calls itself with progressively smaller inputs, thereby breaking down a problem into simpler instances of the same challenge. The key idea behind recursion is that a large, seemingly intractable problem can be reduced to a base case—an easily solvable instance—and a recursive case, where the solution of the current instance relies on the solution of a smaller version of the original problem. This method is particularly effective for tasks such as computing mathematical factorials, traversing data structures like trees, or solving problems that exhibit overlapping subproblems.

A crucial component of recursion is the presence of a base case. This is a condition under which the recursive calls cease, ensuring that the algorithm does not result in an infinite loop. Without a clear base case, the recursive process would continue indefinitely, leading to eventual failure due to resource exhaustion. Therefore, distinguishing between the base and recursive cases is critical. In a recursive function, the base case typically handles the simplest possible input—for example, returning 1 when computing the factorial of 0—while the recursive case handles more complex inputs by calling the function itself with a reduced argument.

```
function factorial(n):
    if n == 0:
        return 1
    else:
        return n * factorial(n - 1)
```

The above code snippet illustrates a simple recursive approach to computing the factorial of a number. In this example, the base case is defined by the condition when n equals zero, ensuring that the recursion terminates. The recursive step reduces the problem size by calling the factorial function with n-1 until eventually reaching the base case. This combination of a clearly defined stopping point and the self-referential nature of the function encapsulates the essence of recursion.

While recursion is elegant and can simplify the implementation of certain problems, iteration is another fundamental strategy widely used in programming. Instead of relying on self-referential function calls, iteration repeatedly executes a block of code until a specified condition is met. Iterative constructs, such as those based on for and while loops, are typically straightforward to understand and implement, making them suitable for a broad range of tasks, from processing items in a list to performing repeated calculations until a convergence criterion is satisfied.

Common iterative constructs include the for loop, which is ideal when the number of iterations is predetermined or when processing each element in a collection; and the while loop, which continues execution based on a condition that is evaluated at each iteration. Each of these constructs offers distinct advantages. For example, the for loop provides clarity when iterating over arrays, while the while loop offers flexibility for scenarios where the termination condition depends on dynamic computations that occur during the loop's execution.

```
function sumList(numbers):
    total = 0
    for number in numbers:
        total = total + number
    return total
```

The above code snippet demonstrates an iterative approach to summing the elements of a list. In this example, the loop iterates over each number in the collection, adding it to a running total, and terminates once all elements have been processed. This type of iterative logic is particularly beneficial when dealing with collections of data where the same operation must be applied to every element.

Divide and conquer is another strategy that has proven its effectiveness in tackling complex problems. This method works by dividing the original problem into several smaller, independent subproblems. Each subproblem is solved separately, often recursively or iteratively, and then the solutions are combined to produce the final result. The strength of the divide and conquer approach lies in its ability to simplify complex tasks by handling smaller, more manageable pieces. This method is particularly prevalent in algorithms such as merge sort, quick sort, and various search algorithms, where the overall efficiency of the algorithm is significantly improved by reducing the problem into smaller segments.

The process of applying divide and conquer typically involves three steps. First, the problem is divided into several smaller subproblems. Second, each of these subproblems is independently conquered by solving them recursively or through other means. Third, the solutions to the subproblems are combined to form the solution for the original problem. This structured process is integral to the success of many high-performing algorithms and illustrates the underlying principle of reducing complexity by addressing simpler tasks.

```
function mergeSort(arr):
    if length(arr) <= 1:
        return arr
    mid = length(arr) // 2
    left = mergeSort(arr[0:mid])
    right = mergeSort(arr[mid:])
    return merge(left, right)

function merge(left, right):
    result = empty list
```

```
while left is not empty and right is not empty:
    if left[0] <= right[0]:
        append left[0] to result
        remove first element from left
    else:
        append right[0] to result
        remove first element from right
while left is not empty:
    append first element of left to result
    remove first element from left
while right is not empty:
    append first element of right to result
    remove first element from right
return result
```

The merge sort algorithm example presented above encapsulates the divide and conquer strategy effectively. Initially, the array is divided into two halves. Each half is independently sorted by recursive calls to the mergeSort function. After achieving sorted subarrays, the merge function combines them, resulting in a fully sorted sequence. This approach illustrates how dividing the problem into simpler components, solving them, and then recombining leads to an efficient overall solution.

A comparison of recursion, iteration, and divide and conquer is instructive for understanding when to use each strategy. Recursion is best suited for problems that naturally exhibit self-similarity, where a problem can be broken down into smaller instances of itself. However, recursive methods may introduce overhead due to multiple function calls and increased memory usage on the call stack, making them less suitable for problems with very deep recursion depths. Iteration, on the other hand, is straightforward and generally more memory efficient. It is ideal for problems where repetitive tasks occur with uniform operations, as it avoids the potential stack overflow issues associated with recursion. Divide and conquer leverages the strengths of recursion and iteration by breaking down problems into independent parts that can be processed concurrently or sequentially, leading to scalable solutions that are particularly effective in sorting, searching, and processing large datasets.

Each of these strategies comes with its own set of advantages and trade-offs. For instance, recursion often results in simpler and more human-readable code, but may require careful handling of base cases to avoid infinite loops. Iteration, while conceptually simpler and usually more efficient in terms of memory usage, might lead to more complex loop constructs when handling intricate problems. Divide and conquer offers a balance by simplifying complex computations through problem partitioning, though it requires additional effort to combine the results effectively. The optimal approach is highly context-dependent, based on factors such as the size of the input, memory constraints, and the nature of the problem being solved.

The integration of these fundamental strategies into programming practice not only enhances problem-solving capabilities but also serves as a foundation for more advanced algorithm design techniques. When evaluating which strategy to adopt, it is essential for programmers to consider the problem's structure and constraints. Problems with a clear self-similar structure are candidates for recursive solutions. Tasks that involve routine iterations across collections or datasets benefit from iterative loops, while large-scale problems that can be decomposed into independent tasks are ideal for the divide and conquer approach.

Moreover, the practical implementation of these strategies often involves a hybrid approach. For example, complex algorithms such as quicksort may initially employ recursion to partition the dataset, followed by iteration to handle smaller subarrays more efficiently. The flexible application of these strategies underscores the importance of understanding their underlying principles to adapt to a wide variety of computational challenges.

Programming environments and languages frequently offer built-in support for these strategies. Many programming constructs allow for elegant recursion, robust iteration, and efficient divide and conquer operations, enabling developers to implement solutions that are both efficient and maintainable. Understanding the strengths and limitations of each method is paramount; it allows programmers to make informed choices that optimize both code clarity and performance. In addition, the process of selecting the right strategy reinforces the practice of analyzing performance aspects such as time complexity and memory consumption—key factors in algorithm design and software development.

Ultimately, the thoughtful application of recursion, iteration, and divide and conquer in solving problems represents a critical aspect of algorithm design. By systematically breaking down problems, developers can achieve solutions that are not only correct but also efficient and scalable. This multifaceted approach is indicative of sound programming practice and serves as a stepping stone to more advanced computational techniques. Moreover, the blend of these fundamental strategies encourages a deeper exploration of problem structure and algorithmic efficiency, fostering a disciplined approach to software development.

The methodologies discussed here form a cornerstone of programming education. They provide a structured framework that guides the transformation of complex ideas into executable code, while also facilitating the debugging and optimization processes. A comprehensive understanding of these strategies empowers learners to tackle diverse problems and adapt their solutions as challenges evolve. Through iterative refinement and careful analysis, programmers can build robust systems that perform reliably under varying conditions, thereby advancing the overall quality of software systems.

Fostering the capacity to evaluate and select the most appropriate problem-solving strategy is essential for both novice and experienced programmers. The insights gathered from examining recursion, iteration, and divide and conquer not only contribute to effective algorithm design but also inspire a mindset rooted in analytical rigor and creative solution development. Embracing these methods in everyday coding practice enhances the ability to construct clear, logical, and efficient solutions that stand the test of both academic inquiry and practical application.

2.3   Asymptotic Analysis

Asymptotic analysis is a fundamental tool used to evaluate the performance of algorithms as the size of their input increases. This form of analysis abstracts away constant factors and lower-order terms in order to focus on the dominant elements that dictate an algorithm's behavior when processing large datasets. With the goal of understanding how algorithms scale, asymptotic analysis provides insight into the efficiency of different approaches, enabling developers to make informed design decisions that balance time and space constraints.

Growth rates form the cornerstone of asymptotic analysis, as they quantify how runtime or memory usage increases with input size. In practice, growth rates offer a mathematical way to compare algorithms by describing their performance trends. For instance, an algorithm whose runtime grows linearly with the input size is fundamentally different from one whose performance degrades quadratically. Understanding these differences is crucial for selecting the appropriate approach for a given problem, particularly when dealing with large-scale applications.

One of the most widely used notations in asymptotic analysis is Big O notation. Big O notation characterizes the worst-case performance of an algorithm by focusing on an upper bound on its growth rate. Essentially, Big O tells us how the runtime of an algorithm increases relative to the input size in the most pessimistic scenario, ensuring that an algorithm will never exceed this bound regardless of the specific input conditions. For example, an algorithm that performs a constant number of operations, regardless of input size, is classified as $O(1)$, while an algorithm that requires time proportional to the number of input elements is classified as $O(n)$. More computationally intensive algorithms, such as those performing nested loops, may exhibit growth rates of $O(n^2)$ or worse.

In addition to Big O notation, Big Theta notation offers a more precise description by representing a tight bound on an algorithm's growth rate. When an algorithm's performance is expressed using Big Theta, it means that the algorithm's runtime will grow at the same rate, both in the best-case and worst-case scenarios, for sufficiently large input sizes. Big Theta thus provides both an upper and lower bound, indicating that the algorithm's behavior is consistent and predictable. Conversely, Big Omega notation is used to denote a lower bound, describing the best-case performance scenario. While Big Omega guarantees a minimum level of performance, it does not exclude the possibility of the algorithm taking longer in other conditions.

Common examples of these notations help to solidify their meaning.

Consider a simple algorithm that retrieves an element from an array: since this operation is performed in constant time regardless of the array's size, it is rated as $O(1)$, $\Theta(1)$, and $\Omega(1)$. In contrast, an algorithm that iterates through every element in a list to find a specific value exhibits linear growth, generally expressed as $O(n)$ for the worst-case scenario. A more complex example is a nested loop on an array, where the runtime grows quadratically relative to the size of the array; such an algorithm would be classified as $O(n^2)$. These standard examples illustrate how different algorithms scale in response to input size and why selecting the right algorithm relies heavily on understanding these growth patterns.

To further clarify these concepts, one can visualize asymptotic notations using a graphical representation. Consider the following table, which contrasts Big O, Big Theta, and Big Omega in terms of their descriptions and growth rates:

Notation	Description	Growth Rate Behavior
Big O (O)	Upper bound on runtime	Worst-case scenario; may overestimate actual growth
Big Theta (Θ)	Tight bound on runtime	Exact asymptotic behavior; both upper and lower bounds
Big Omega (Ω)	Lower bound on runtime	Best-case scenario; guarantees minimum performance

Table 2.2: *Graphical Comparison of Asymptotic Notations*

This table encapsulates the primary distinctions among the three notations. Big O provides a guarantee against exceeding a certain growth rate, Big Theta matches the algorithm's precise behavior in all cases, and Big Omega ensures that the algorithm operates above a certain threshold in the best-case scenario.

In addition to these foundational notations, amortized analysis is another critical component of asymptotic analysis that averages the cost of operations through a sequence of actions. Amortized analysis is particularly useful when assessing data structure operations that occasionally incur high costs but generally perform at a low rate. For example, while inserting an element into a dynamic array might sometimes require resizing the array (an expensive operation), amortized analysis shows that the average cost per insertion is low over a long sequence of operations. This perspective is valuable because it offers a more nuanced understanding of algorithm performance that goes beyond worst-case estimates.

Despite its usefulness, asymptotic analysis has several common pitfalls that practitioners must be aware of. One such pitfall is the neglect of lower order terms and constant factors which, although insignificant for very large inputs, may still have practical implications for moderate input sizes or in systems with strict performance requirements. Another frequent error is over-reliance on worst-case analysis provided by Big O notation without considering average and best-case scenarios, as described by Big Theta and Big Omega, respectively. Furthermore, failing to account for the amortized cost of occasional expensive operations can lead to misconceptions about an algorithm's overall efficiency. To avoid these mistakes, it is important to thoroughly analyze algorithms across different scenarios and input sizes, and to use a combination of notational perspectives to achieve a balanced view of performance.

When comparing algorithms, asymptotic analysis serves as an essential tool for identifying bottlenecks and guiding the design process. It enables developers to understand why one algorithm might perform better than another and how those differences become significant as the input grows. By focusing on the highest order term, asymptotic analysis abstracts away implementation-specific details and highlights the fundamental computational complexity. This abstraction is critical when scaling applications, as it assists in predicting performance under heavy workloads and in identifying cases where algorithmic improvements are necessary.

Understanding asymptotic notation is not only a theoretical exercise but also a practical one. With large datasets and ever-increasing performance demands, modern software systems must be designed with scalability in mind. Through asymptotic analysis, developers can estimate runtime and memory demands, allowing for more robust system architectures that accommodate growth. For example, when designing a search engine that deals with massive amounts of data, knowing that a particular algorithm operates in $O(\log n)$ time rather than $O(n)$ can be the determining factor in success. Similarly, in situations where real-time performance is critical, such as in embedded systems or financial trading platforms, a clear understanding of asymptotic behavior can be the difference between meeting performance targets and system failure.

Moreover, the integration of asymptotic analysis into algorithm design encourages a systematic approach to optimization. As developers confront a problem, they can use these notations to guide their decisions regarding which algorithmic strategies to employ and which bottlenecks to address first. Optimizing algorithms based on their asymptotic behavior facilitates the design of software that not only functions correctly but also performs efficiently under a broad range of conditions. This approach is essential for developing high-quality software that scales with increasing data volume and complexity.

It is important to emphasize that asymptotic analysis, while powerful, does not provide a complete picture on its own. Practical considerations, such as hardware characteristics, caching mechanisms, and compiler optimizations, can influence the actual performance of a program. Therefore, while theoretical analysis using Big O, Big Theta, and Big Omega offers invaluable insights, it should be complemented by empirical testing and profiling. By combining theoretical benchmarks with practical measurements, developers can validate their expectations and fine-tune their implementations for optimal performance.

Asymptotic analysis offers a rigorous framework for evaluating how algorithms perform as input sizes grow. By using Big O notation, developers can understand the worst-case scenario, while Big Theta and Big Omega provide a more balanced view by describing tight and lower bounds, respectively. The incorporation of graphical tools such as the provided table further aids in clarifying these concepts. Integrating amortized analysis enriches the assessment by smoothing out the cost of occasional high-latency operations. A critical understanding of potential pitfalls, such as ignoring lower order terms or relying solely on worst-case estimates, ensures that developers maintain a comprehensive view of algorithm efficiency. Ultimately, asymptotic analysis drives software design decisions by emphasizing scalability and performance, guiding developers toward creating robust, efficient algorithms that meet the demands of modern computing environments.

2.4 Evaluating Efficiency

Understanding the efficiency of an algorithm is crucial for assessing its practical performance in real-world applications. Evaluating efficiency involves analyzing both runtime and memory usage, which together determine how well an algorithm performs in processing data. Efficiency evaluation not only impacts the speed of the software but also dictates how much computing resource is required. As input sizes grow, inefficient algorithms may lead to unacceptable delays or resource consumption, thus making a thorough performance evaluation an indispensable part of the design and implementation process.

Runtime analysis is one key aspect of efficiency evaluation. This analysis examines how the execution time of an algorithm increases as the size of the input expands. The primary goal is to understand an algorithm's temporal behavior under varying conditions and to predict its performance in both worst-case and average-case scenarios. Runtime analysis usually involves both theoretical assessments, such as asymptotic analysis using Big O notation, and practical measurements that capture the actual execution time. Theoretical methods offer general insights by abstracting away machine-specific constants and lower order factors, while empirical measurements provide real-world validation.

Measuring runtime has several approaches. Theoretical techniques include analyzing the number of fundamental operations based on algorithm structure. For instance, an algorithm with nested loops may exhibit quadratic behavior in the worst-case scenario, while others might work in linear or logarithmic time. Experimental approaches, on the other hand, involve running the algorithm on different data sizes using timers or benchmark libraries. These experiments may be repeated several times to account for variability in processing conditions and to arrive at average runtime estimates. Such techniques help compare expected performance with observed performance, providing a comprehensive view of an algorithm's behavior.

Empirical testing techniques further enhance the evaluation process. One common method is benchmarking, where specific tests are conducted under controlled conditions to measure execution times. Using high-precision timers, developers can record the duration of critical operations. In addition, profiling tools allow developers to monitor different parts of an algorithm, identifying bottlenecks and inefficient sections. Profilers typically capture detailed metrics such as the number of function calls, CPU cycles, and even cache misses. This information is valuable for pinpointing performance limitations and optimizing the code.

In tandem with runtime, memory usage analysis is essential to understand how much working storage an algorithm requires during execution. Memory efficiency is particularly important in applications with limited resources or in systems where multiple processes compete for memory. Memory usage analysis explores how the storage space requirements evolve with increasing input sizes. This overview often involves studying the space complexity of an algorithm, which indicates the amount of memory consumed relative to the input, and is typically expressed using asymptotic notations similar to those used in runtime analysis.

Measuring memory consumption can be as critical as measuring execution time. Techniques for assessing memory usage include instrumentation of the code to monitor allocation and deallocation events. Tools that profile memory usage track variables, data structures, and heap allocation, providing a detailed snapshot of how the memory footprint changes over time. For example, static code analysis can offer insights into potential memory leaks, while dynamic analysis with profilers reveals real-time memory consumption. Such insights help ensure that an algorithm not only runs quickly but also optimally allocates resources and avoids unnecessary clutter.

A fundamental concept in discussing memory usage is space complexity. Space complexity quantifies the amount of extra memory needed by an algorithm as a function of the input size. It distinguishes between the space required for the input itself and additional space required for processing, such as temporary arrays or data structures. An algorithm that consumes memory proportional to the size of the input is said to have linear space complexity, whereas one that requires a fixed amount of extra memory—irrespective of the input—is classified as having constant space complexity. Understanding space complexity is critical because even if an algorithm executes quickly, its real-world applicability might be limited by excessive memory demands.

Trade-offs between time and space further complicate performance evaluation. In many cases, optimizing for runtime may incur additional memory usage, and vice versa. For instance, a solution employing memoization stores intermediate results to avoid redundant computations, effectively reducing the runtime complexity at the potential cost of increased memory usage. Conversely, an algorithm designed to use minimal memory might need to recompute certain values, thereby extending its execution time. Such trade-offs require a careful balance, and the optimal solution generally depends on the specific constraints of the application environment. When designing an algorithm, it is crucial to understand and manage these trade-offs so that the implemented solution is both fast and memory-efficient.

Profiling tools and techniques have become vital in modern software development as they help developers monitor and improve both runtime and memory performance. Tools such as gprof, Valgrind, and Visual Studio Profiler provide detailed insights into how code performs under various circumstances. These tools can highlight functions with excessive runtime, flag memory leaks, and even suggest where code optimizations can yield significant performance improvements. By employing these profiling tools, developers can ensure that the software

59

meets performance benchmarks and scales appropriately with usage.

A practical example that illustrates these performance considerations involves a case study comparing two algorithms for solving the same problem. Suppose we are evaluating two approaches to searching a list: a simple linear search and a more sophisticated binary search. In a linear search, the algorithm examines each element in sequence until the target is found or the list is exhausted, leading to a worst-case runtime that increases linearly with the size of the list. In contrast, binary search operates on a sorted list by repeatedly dividing the search interval in half, resulting in a logarithmic growth rate in the worst-case scenario. While binary search typically requires a pre-sorted list (which may itself introduce a runtime overhead and additional memory usage), the efficiency gain in search operations is significant for large datasets. Empirical testing can involve measuring the execution times of both algorithms over multiple iterations with varying input sizes, and memory profiling can reveal any associated resource overhead. Such empirical comparisons provide practical evidence on why algorithm selection and design must account for both runtime and memory consumption to achieve optimal performance.

The evaluation of efficiency is not merely an academic exercise—it has direct implications for real-world software performance. As systems scale and data volumes increase, the ability of algorithms to manage time and memory becomes a critical factor determining overall system performance. Developers must consider not just the theoretical complexity of algorithms but also the practical aspects of how they perform under load. Profiling, benchmarking, and memory analysis are integral to this process, ensuring that performance bottlenecks are identified and addressed early in the development cycle.

Evaluating algorithm efficiency encompasses both runtime analysis and memory usage analysis. Runtime analysis involves understanding how the duration of an algorithm's execution scales with the input size, employing theoretical and empirical methods to capture performance. Memory usage analysis focuses on the space requirements, using techniques that range from static analysis to dynamic profiling. Together, these assessments reveal the trade-offs inherent in algorithm design, where improvements in speed might come at the cost of increased memory consumption, and vice versa. By leveraging profiling tools and conducting thorough case studies, developers are equipped to make informed decisions that optimize both speed and resource utilization. Ultimately, a balanced approach to efficiency evaluation is essential for building robust, scalable, and high-performing software systems that satisfy real-world constraints and user demands.

2.5   Time vs Space Trade-offs

Analyzing the balance between time complexity and space complexity is crucial in algorithm design, as it directly impacts the performance and practicality of software systems. Time complexity measures how the running time of an algorithm increases relative to the input size, while space complexity evaluates the amount of memory required during execution. These metrics are indispensable in evaluating algorithm performance because real-world applications must satisfy requirements for both speed and memory efficiency under varying constraints and conditions.

Time complexity essentially quantifies the duration an algorithm takes to complete its task given a particular input, often expressed using asymptotic notations such as O, Θ, and Ω. For example, an algorithm that examines each element of an array once displays a linear time complexity, denoted as $O(n)$, meaning that the execution time grows proportionally with the number of elements. On the other hand, algorithms with nested loops might result in quadratic time complexity, $O(n^2)$, reflecting a significant increase in running time with larger inputs. Understanding these patterns allows developers to predict performance and choose a strategy that best meets the operational constraints of the intended environment.

In parallel, space complexity serves as an indicator of the memory resources an algorithm requires during its execution, including both the space for inputs and additional working storage such as temporary variables and data structures. For instance, an algorithm that utilizes a fixed-size data structure irrespective of the input size is considered to have constant space complexity, $O(1)$. Conversely, an algorithm that copies an input array into a new array will typically have linear space complexity, $O(n)$, as the memory requirement scales directly with the size of the input. Evaluating space complexity is especially important in scenarios with limited memory resources or when multiple algorithms run concurrently.

Trade-offs between time and space complexity are a common phenomenon in software development. Practical examples illustrate that optimizing for a faster runtime may sometimes lead to higher memory usage and vice versa. One widely used technique that embodies this trade-off is caching or memoization. By storing the results of expensive function calls, memoization can significantly reduce redundant computations, thus improving runtime performance. However, the trade-off is that storing these intermediate results increases the memory footprint of the program. For example, a recursive algorithm that computes Fibonacci numbers can use memoization to avoid repeated calculations, thereby converting an exponential time algorithm into a linear one, while it requires additional memory for the cache. This strategy is often beneficial in systems where runtime performance is prioritized over memory constraints.

On the other side of the spectrum, space-efficient algorithms are designed to minimize memory usage, which is essential for applications operating under tight memory restrictions. Techniques for designing space-efficient algorithms may include in-place modifications to data structures, using minimal auxiliary storage, or applying iterative methods instead of recursion when possible. Although these techniques can result in lower memory consumption, they may sometimes come at the cost of increased running time. For example, an in-place sorting algorithm such as insertion sort uses little additional memory; however, its time complexity is higher when compared to more memory-intensive algorithms like merge sort. This demonstrates that the choice of algorithm often depends on whether the application demands faster execution or lower memory usage.

Conversely, time-efficient algorithms are geared towards achieving rapid execution, even if that means using more memory. These algorithms typically incorporate extra data structures, such as hash tables or precomputed lookup arrays, to bypass time-consuming calculations. A classic example is the use of dynamic programming to solve problems that have overlapping subproblems. By storing the solutions to these subproblems in a table, dynamic programming significantly reduces unnecessary recomputation, leading to faster overall performance. However, the additional memory allocated for the table represents an increased space complexity. Thus, the decision to use a time-efficient algorithm must consider whether the available system resources can handle the extra memory demand.

Real-world considerations further complicate the balance between time and space. Hardware limitations, such as available physical memory and processing power, directly influence the suitability of an algorithm for a particular application. In environments with limited memory, such as embedded systems or mobile devices, a space-efficient algorithm might be preferred even if it results in slower runtime. In contrast, server-side applications handling large volumes of transactions may favor time efficiency, where added memory usage is acceptable if it leads to a faster response. Additionally, application requirements such as responsiveness in interactive systems or throughput in data processing pipelines may tip the balance toward one metric over the other. Consequently, developers must analyze the constraints of the target environment and determine which trade-off is more acceptable for the task at hand.

Practical examples in software development showcase these trade-offs in action. Consider a scenario where a developer must choose between two data structures for managing a dynamic collection of items: one that offers faster search capabilities but requires additional memory, and another that is more memory-efficient but offers slower access times. In a database indexing scenario, where quick retrieval of records is critical, the developer might choose a data structure that consumes more memory to ensure rapid query responses. Alternatively, in a mobile application where memory is at a premium, a space-optimized structure, even if slightly slower, could be the better choice. These examples underscore that real-world applications often necessitate a nuanced evaluation of algorithm performance that cannot be captured by a single metric.

Profiling tools and techniques are invaluable for analyzing these trade-offs. Developers use profilers to gather detailed information about an algorithm's runtime behavior and memory consumption. Tools like GNU gprof, Valgrind, and Visual Studio Profiler provide insights into which functions or code segments consume the most resources. Profiling not only helps in identifying bottlenecks but also assists in visualizing the impact of different design choices. For example, by comparing the performance of a recursive algorithm with a memoized version, developers can quantify the improvement in execution time alongside the increase in memory usage. This empirical data supports informed decision-making and allows for a more targeted optimization of both time and space efficiency.

In many cases, analyzing the trade-offs involves detailed benchmarking. By systematically varying input sizes and measuring the corresponding changes in runtime and memory usage, developers can create performance models that predict how the algorithm scales. These models help in identifying thresholds where an algorithm's performance might degrade or where memory usage becomes a limiting factor. Furthermore, benchmarking under realistic conditions, which mimic the actual operating environment, ensures that the theoretical improvements translate into tangible benefits when the system is deployed.

Another aspect of evaluating these trade-offs is understanding that different phases of an algorithm might have distinct efficiency considerations. For instance, an algorithm may perform a pre-processing step that consumes substantial memory to organize data in a structure that supports faster queries during later stages. The overall performance is then a combination of the one-time memory and time investment during pre-processing and the subsequent improvements in query efficiency. This layered approach emphasizes that trade-offs are not always directly opposed; rather, they can be orchestrated strategically to balance overall system performance.

In designing efficient algorithms, developers often make iterative refinements to achieve an optimal balance between time and space. Initial designs may be focused on correctness, followed by profiling to identify performance issues. Subsequent iterations might involve experimenting with different data structures, caching strategies, or algorithmic paradigms to improve speed without significantly increasing memory overhead. During this process, trade-offs are continuously reevaluated as deeper insights into the application's behavior under load are obtained.

Furthermore, the interplay among time, space, and other factors such as energy consumption or network latency adds additional layers of complexity. For instance, in distributed systems, reducing the time complexity of an algorithm may lead to increased communication overhead or memory usage across networked nodes. Similarly, in energy-constrained environments, such as battery-operated devices, the trade-off between rapid computation and low power consumption becomes paramount. These broader considerations highlight that algorithm efficiency evaluation extends beyond mere computation and requires a comprehensive understanding of all system resources.

Ultimately, understanding and managing time versus space trade-offs is a fundamental skill for developing efficient, real-world algorithms. It requires a balanced approach that carefully considers the inherent limitations of the hardware, the specific requirements of the application, and the broader context in which the software will operate. Developers must be adept at recognizing when speed is the priority and when minimizing memory usage is more critical. By combining theoretical analysis with practical profiling and benchmarking, developers can fine-tune their solutions to achieve sustainable performance improvements.

Time and space complexities represent two sides of the same coin in algorithm design, and the art of balancing these trade-offs is central to building efficient software. Through practical examples, profiling, and a deep understanding of underlying hardware constraints, developers can make judicious choices that satisfy both performance demands and resource limitations. This balanced approach not only leads to better-performing algorithms but also ensures that systems can scale gracefully as data volumes and usage patterns evolve over time.

3

Fundamental Data Structures

This chapter explores essential data structures that form the backbone of effective algorithm implementation. It begins by examining arrays and lists, detailing their properties and use cases in storing sequential data. The discussion then moves to stacks and queues, highlighting their LIFO and FIFO principles, respectively, and their practical applications. Readers will also learn about linked data structures, which facilitate dynamic memory allocation and efficient insertion and deletion operations. Finally, the chapter delves into tree and graph structures, emphasizing their importance in organizing hierarchical and networked data for various computational problems.

3.1 Arrays and Lists

Arrays and lists are sequential data structures used to store collections of elements in computer memory. They serve as one of the foundational concepts in programming by organizing data in a structured manner that facilitates efficient access and manipulation. An array typically stores elements in contiguous memory locations, whereas a list can offer more flexibility by allowing dynamic resizing and the ease of inserting or deleting elements. In many programming scenarios, these structures are chosen according to performance considerations and the particular requirements of the task at hand.

Arrays provide a fixed-length structure when declared statically; in this case, memory allocation occurs at compile time and the size of the array cannot change during execution. This property results in efficient memory access because the location of any element can be computed quickly using its index and the base address. By contrast, dynamic arrays allow resizable storage, often by using underlying constructs that automatically manage memory allocation and reallocation. The trade-off with dynamic arrays is that they have additional overhead when resizing, but they provide the flexibility needed in applications where the number of elements cannot be predetermined.

When considering array properties, index-based access is one of the most important aspects. Arrays use indices to access individual elements, making it possible to retrieve any element in constant time, $O(1)$, assuming no bounds checking overhead influences performance. The contiguous memory layout further enhances performance by leveraging spatial locality, which is beneficial for caching mechanisms. Static arrays, defined at compile time, are typically allocated on the stack and offer fast allocation and deallocation, whereas dynamic arrays are usually allocated on the heap. This distinction also affects memory management strategies and has implications for overall application performance.

Providing code examples can further clarify the concepts by illustrating how to create and initialize arrays. In the C++ programming language, for instance, a static array can be declared simply by specifying its size and data type, while a dynamic array can be implemented using standard library containers such as `std::vector`. The following code example demonstrates both approaches:

```cpp
#include <iostream>
#include <vector>

int main() {
    // Static array: fixed size
    int staticArray[5] = {1, 2, 3, 4, 5};

    // Dynamic array using std::vector: size can be modified at runtime
    std::vector<int> dynamicArray = {1, 2, 3, 4, 5};

    // Display elements of the static array
    std::cout << "Static Array: ";
    for (int i = 0; i < 5; i++) {
        std::cout << staticArray[i] << " ";
    }
    std::cout << std::endl;

    // Display elements of the dynamic array
    std::cout << "Dynamic Array: ";
    for (size_t i = 0; i < dynamicArray.size(); i++) {
        std::cout << dynamicArray[i] << " ";
    }
    std::cout << std::endl;

    return 0;
}
```

Accessing and modifying array elements is a straightforward process due to the use of indices. In languages with zero-based indexing, the first element has the index 0, and the last element has the index size - 1. This method of access is efficient and predictable in terms of performance. One must remain vigilant with respect to boundary conditions, as accessing an index outside the declared range can lead to undefined behavior or runtime errors. Additionally, some programming languages implement one-based indexing; understanding the implications of each indexing system is crucial to avoid common off-by-one errors. Modifying an array element is as simple as assigning a new value to a given index, which again, typically operates in constant time.

Common operations performed on arrays include traversal, searching, sorting, and merging. Traversal involves iterating through all elements of the array sequentially, which has a time complexity of $O(n)$ for an array of n elements. Sorting algorithms, such as quicksort or mergesort, are applied to arrange elements in a certain order, with average time complexities ranging from $O(n \log n)$ to $O(n^2)$ in less optimal cases. Searching for an element in an unsorted array usually requires looking at each element, resulting in linear time complexity. However, if the array is sorted, more efficient search algorithms like binary search can be employed with $O(\log n)$ complexity. Merging two arrays or parts of a single array is common in many algorithmic strategies, especially in divide and conquer approaches. Each of these operations impacts overall application performance and must be selected based on the computational resources available and the size of the data set.

While arrays are efficient for fixed-size data sequences, lists provide an alternative that supports dynamic insertion and deletion of elements. Lists, especially those implemented as linked lists, cater to situations where the number of elements is not known in advance or may vary

72

during runtime. A list does not require contiguous memory, and it can easily grow or shrink as elements are added or removed. The structure of a list is typically organized as nodes where each node holds data and a pointer (or link) to the next node in the sequence. This pointer-based approach allows for efficient insertion or deletion at arbitrary positions without the need to shift other elements, as is often necessary with arrays.

In a linked list, each node is the basic building block. The node structure generally consists of one or more data fields and a reference or pointer to the next node. In a singly linked list, each node points only to the next node in the sequence, which simplifies the design and reduces memory overhead. However, this design provides only one-directional traversal. Doubly linked lists extend this idea by having pointers both to the next node and the previous node, enabling bidirectional traversal. Despite the increased memory requirements and complexity in pointer manipulation, doubly linked lists offer more flexibility in certain applications.

An illustrative example of creating and manipulating a linked list in C++ is shown below. This code sample demonstrates how to define a simple node structure, create a linked list, and perform basic operations such as insertion at the head and deletion of elements.

```
#include <iostream>

// Define the structure of a Node for a singly linked list.
struct Node {
    int data;
    Node* next;
};

// Function to insert a new node at the head of the list.
void insertAtHead(Node*& head, int value) {
    Node* newNode = new Node;
```

```
        newNode->data = value;
        newNode->next = head;
        head = newNode;
}


// Function to delete a node with a given value from the list.
void deleteNode(Node*& head, int value) {
    if (!head) return;
    if (head->data == value) {
        Node* temp = head;
        head = head->next;
        delete temp;
        return;
    }
    Node* current = head;
    while (current->next && current->next->data != value) {
        current = current->next;
    }
    if (current->next) {
        Node* temp = current->next;
        current->next = current->next->next;
        delete temp;
    }
}


// Function to print the linked list.
void printList(Node* head) {
    while (head) {
        std::cout << head->data << " -> ";
        head = head->next;
    }
    std::cout << "NULL" << std::endl;
}


int main() {
    Node* head = nullptr;
    insertAtHead(head, 3);
    insertAtHead(head, 2);
    insertAtHead(head, 1);

    std::cout << "Linked List: ";
    printList(head);

    deleteNode(head, 2);
    std::cout << "After deletion: ";
```

74

```
    printList(head);

    // Clean up the remaining nodes
    while (head) {
        Node* temp = head;
        head = head->next;
        delete temp;
    }
    return 0;
}
```

Arrays and lists are utilized in various practical settings to solve common data storage problems. For instance, arrays are well-suited for applications where fast, random access is required and the number of elements remains constant. They are widely used in embedded systems and scenarios where the overhead of dynamic memory allocation is undesirable. Conversely, lists, with their dynamic nature, are advantageous in applications that involve frequent insertions and deletions, such as in certain types of databases or when implementing queues and stacks. The choice between arrays and lists is highly dependent on the specific use case, as arrays provide efficient access and better cache performance, while lists offer flexibility in memory management and growth.

In many software systems, data storage needs vary significantly. Simple databases, for example, may initially use arrays for efficient indexed access but later switch to list-based structures when the need for dynamic data handling becomes apparent. Lists are also a preferred structure when implementing complex data models that require non-contiguous memory storage. The selection between these data structures often comes down to analyzing the trade-offs: static arrays come with predictable memory usage and performance while dynamic arrays offer variability with a possible cost in terms of runtime overhead during resizing processes. Similarly, linked lists allow for dynamic size management but may incur extra processing time due to pointer management during element traversal.

The performance characteristics of arrays and lists continue to be a focal point when making design decisions. Arrays, due to their contiguous block of memory allocation, excel in scenarios where predictable and constant time access to any element is crucial. In contrast, lists are optimal when the operations performed mostly involve inserting or removing elements, and the overhead of shifting elements in an array becomes significant. The analysis of these structures frequently involves considerations about worst-case, average-case, and best-case scenarios, largely dependent on the underlying hardware architecture and the programming language's runtime environment. Both arrays and lists are indispensable components in the broader context of algorithm design and implementation, each offering specialized benefits that can be leveraged in solving various computational problems.

The fundamental differences between arrays and lists become evident when directly comparing their performance characteristics and use cases. Arrays shine in environments requiring quick, random access and efficient memory usage when the number of data points is predetermined or does not change frequently. Lists, particularly in the form of linked implementations, offer superior flexibility when the dataset is subject to frequent modifications. Overall, arrays and lists collectively form the basis for many complex algorithms and data handling techniques. Their proper usage is critical not only for basic data storage but also for the efficiency and scalability of software systems.

The foundational aspects of arrays and lists play a critical role in understanding more advanced data structures and algorithms. Mastery of these sequential structures enables the design and implementation of efficient code and paves the way for exploring more complex data storage methods. By grasping the nuances of static versus dynamic arrays, the principles of index-based access, and the benefits of linked list architectures, programmers establish a robust groundwork that is essential for developing sophisticated software systems.

3.2   Stacks and Queues

Stacks and queues are fundamental data structures that model two distinct methods for storing and retrieving data, each tailored for specific computational tasks. A stack is characterized by the Last In First Out (LIFO) principle, which means that the most recently added element is the first one to be removed. Conversely, a queue implements the First In First Out (FIFO) strategy where elements are removed in the exact order they were added. These concepts form the cornerstone of many algorithmic solutions and system operations, ranging from managing function calls to scheduling tasks.

Stacks are constructed as linear structures where elements are added (pushed) onto the top of the stack and removed (popped) from the same position. The operations associated with stacks include push, pop, and peek, each of which can typically be performed in constant time, $O(1)$. The push operation appends a new element to the end of the sequence, while the pop operation removes the element that was most recently added. The peek operation allows one to inspect the top element without altering the structure of the stack. In many programming paradigms, particularly in the context of function call management in recursion, stacks are essential because they provide a reliable method for tracking execution progress and returning control

77

to previous states.

The implementation of stack operations involves careful consideration of memory allocation and error checking. For example, a stack may be implemented using an array or a linked list, and both approaches have their own trade-offs. Array-based stacks offer fast access to elements, but are typically constrained by a fixed size unless dynamic resizing is used. Linked list-based stacks, however, provide flexibility with dynamic allocation but may incur the overhead of additional memory for pointer storage. The simplicity of the stack operations belies the depth of their applications, especially in contexts such as expression evaluation, backtracking algorithms, and undo mechanisms in software applications.

A practical implementation of a stack can be demonstrated using a beginner-friendly programming language. The following code snippet written in Python illustrates the basic operations associated with a stack:

```python
class Stack:
    def __init__(self):
        self.items = []  # Initialize the stack with an empty list

    def push(self, item):
        self.items.append(item)  # Append item to the end of the list

    def pop(self):
        if not self.is_empty():
            return self.items.pop()  # Remove and return the last item
        raise IndexError("pop from empty stack")

    def peek(self):
        if not self.is_empty():
            return self.items[-1]  # Return the last item without removal
        raise IndexError("peek from empty stack")

    def is_empty(self):
        return len(self.items) == 0
```

78

```
# Example usage of the stack
if __name__ == "__main__":
    stack = Stack()
    stack.push(10)
    stack.push(20)
    stack.push(30)
    print("Top of the stack:", stack.peek())   # Output: 30
    print("Popped element:", stack.pop())       # Output: 30
    print("New top after pop:", stack.peek())   # Output: 20
```

This example encapsulates the basic stack operations in an accessible manner, illustrating how elements can be added, inspected, and removed. The use of conditional checks in the 'pop' and 'peek' methods ensures that errors are managed suitably by raising an exception when an attempt is made to operate on an empty stack.

Queues, in contrast, adhere to the FIFO principle. In a queue, new elements are added to the end of the sequence (enqueued), and the removal of elements occurs from the beginning (dequeued). This structure is analogously similar to waiting lines in everyday scenarios: the first person in line is served first. The fundamental operations of a queue include enqueue, dequeue, front, and isEmpty. Enqueuing an element is generally an $O(1)$ operation, and if implemented correctly (for example, using a circular array or a linked list), dequeuing can also be achieved in constant time. However, careful implementation is necessary to avoid inefficient memory usage or time-consuming element shifting.

Queues have a range of applications including task scheduling, buffer management, and network data handling. For instance, operating systems utilize queues to manage processes, while simulations often employ queues to model lines or waiting structures. Similarly to stacks, queues can be implemented using arrays or linked lists. Array-based queues can suffer from inefficiencies when elements are shifted upon each dequeue operation unless a circular queue design is applied. Linked list implementations, on the other hand, maintain a reference to both the head and tail of the list, allowing for efficient enqueuing and dequeuing operations.

A sample implementation of a queue in Python that demonstrates these operations is presented below:

```python
class Queue:
    def __init__(self):
        self.items = []  # Initialize the queue with an empty list

    def enqueue(self, item):
        self.items.append(item)  # Add item to the end of the queue

    def dequeue(self):
        if not self.is_empty():
            return self.items.pop(0)  # Remove and return the first item
        raise IndexError("dequeue from empty queue")

    def front(self):
        if not self.is_empty():
            return self.items[0]  # Return the first item without removal
        raise IndexError("front from empty queue")

    def is_empty(self):
        return len(self.items) == 0

# Example usage of the queue
if __name__ == "__main__":
    queue = Queue()
    queue.enqueue(100)
    queue.enqueue(200)
    queue.enqueue(300)
    print("Front of the queue:", queue.front())  # Output: 100
    print("Dequeued element:", queue.dequeue())    # Output: 100
    print("New front after dequeue:", queue.front()) # Output: 200
```

This code snippet demonstrates how a queue can be implemented using a Python list. The operations for enqueuing and dequeuing are provided with proper error checking, ensuring that any attempt to access an element from an empty queue produces an appropriate error. The function 'front' allows the user to view the next element to be dequeued without modifying the queue's state. The simplicity of this example makes queues accessible to beginners, while also highlighting their practical applications in task management and scheduling.

In many real-world applications, stacks and queues are indispensable. Stacks are often used in scenarios where undo operations are required, such as in text editors or feature-rich software applications. They are also critical in handling function calls in recursive algorithms where the call stack maintains execution context. Queues, on the other hand, find their use in a wide variety of settings. For example, in managing system resources, operating systems rely on queues to allocate CPU time to processes. They are also prevalent in networking, where data packets are buffered in queues before being processed. Moreover, queues can be used in simulation models and real-time event handling systems, where the order of operations is essential for accurate outcomes.

When comparing stacks and queues, their operational differences become apparent. Stacks provide rapid access to the most recent element, making them suitable for problems where the order of operations is inverted relative to the order of insertion. This is fundamental in the evaluation of expressions or backtracking problems. Queues, conversely, process elements in the order they arrive, thereby ensuring fairness and predictability in service. The choice between these data structures is not arbitrary; it is dictated by the particular requirements of the algorithm or system being developed. For instance, a function call manager will almost invariably use a stack to handle nested calls, while a print

81

spooler in an operating system will implement a queue to ensure that print jobs are processed in the order they are received.

Performance considerations play a significant role in deciding which structure to use. Stack operations, being single-pointer manipulations at one end of the data structure, are typically extremely efficient and can be implemented with very low overhead. Queue operations may introduce additional overhead if not implemented with an efficient underlying mechanism to handle shifting elements or if the structure does not support circular buffering. Both structures, when implemented correctly, ensure that the worst-case time complexities for their essential operations remain constant.

From an educational standpoint, understanding stacks and queues is critical before progressing to more complex data structures such as trees and graphs. Their simplicity, combined with a wide range of applications, makes them valuable for teaching key programming paradigms like memory management, pointer manipulation, and the importance of order in computing processes. Furthermore, practical experience with these data structures facilitates a deeper comprehension of algorithms that rely on internal mechanisms similar to stacks and queues.

Stacks and queues continue to lay the groundwork for advanced algorithmic strategies and system designs. In many software solutions, these structures are often combined with other data structures to form hybrid systems that leverage the strengths of each. For example, parsing expressions in compilers may use a combination of stacks for handling operators and queues for managing tokens, demonstrating that the principles of LIFO and FIFO are versatile and applicable beyond isolated tasks.

The exploration of stacks and queues reinforces the importance of choosing the appropriate data structure for a given problem. It is essential for beginners to appreciate how the method of element storage and retrieval can significantly influence algorithm efficiency and system performance. By understanding the underlying principles of LIFO and FIFO, programmers are better equipped to design systems that are both robust and optimized for their intended applications. The detailed examination of these structures—from conceptual definitions and operational characteristics to code implementations and practical use cases—demonstrates their pivotal role in the landscape of computer science.

3.3 Linked Data Structures

Linked data structures are fundamental constructs that organize data into discrete units called nodes and their corresponding connections, providing dynamic memory allocation capabilities that overcome the limitations of static arrays. Unlike arrays, which require contiguous memory allocation and a fixed size determined at compile time, linked data structures allow for flexible growth and contraction during runtime without the necessity of reallocating or copying the entire dataset. This dynamic quality makes linked structures particularly advantageous in cases where the total number of elements is not known in advance or changes frequently over the execution of a program.

A node is the core component of a linked data structure. Each node typically consists of at least one data field and one or more pointer references that establish links with other nodes. The simplest form of a node contains a single data element and a pointer to the next node in

83

a sequence. This pointer-based linkage is what enables the creation of lists that are not bound by contiguous storage in memory. The physical memory layout of nodes can be scattered throughout the system; however, logical organization is maintained via pointers that connect nodes in the intended order. This design emphasizes flexibility and efficient use of memory, even though it may come at the cost of additional overhead in pointer storage.

Singly linked lists are one of the most basic types of linked data structures. In a singly linked list, each node contains a data value and a single pointer that links it to the next node. This structure facilitates one-directional traversal, meaning that one can only navigate from the beginning of the list toward the end. The operations associated with singly linked lists include insertion, deletion, and traversal, all of which can be implemented in a relatively straightforward manner. Insertion typically involves adjusting the pointer of the preceding node to reference a newly created node, while deletion requires bypassing the node to be removed by linking its predecessor to its successor. Although these operations are efficient in terms of time complexity when performed at the beginning or middle of the list, searching for a specific element necessitates sequential traversal, resulting in linear time complexity.

The following code snippet demonstrates the basic operations involved in creating and manipulating a singly linked list. In this example, functions are provided to insert a new node at the beginning of the list, to delete a node with a specified value, and to traverse the list to print its contents:

```
#include <iostream>

// Definition for singly linked list node.
struct Node {
```

```
    int data;
    Node* next;
};


// Insert a new node at the beginning of the list.
void insertAtHead(Node*& head, int value) {
    Node* newNode = new Node;
    newNode->data = value;
    newNode->next = head;
    head = newNode;
}


// Delete the first node with the specified value.
void deleteNode(Node*& head, int value) {
    if (!head) return;
    if (head->data == value) {
        Node* temp = head;
        head = head->next;
        delete temp;
        return;
    }
    Node* current = head;
    while (current->next && current->next->data != value) {
        current = current->next;
    }
    if (current->next) {
        Node* temp = current->next;
        current->next = current->next->next;
        delete temp;
    }
}


// Traverse and print the list.
void traverseList(Node* head) {
    while (head) {
        std::cout << head->data << " -> ";
        head = head->next;
    }
    std::cout << "NULL" << std::endl;
}


int main() {
    Node* head = nullptr;
    insertAtHead(head, 10);
    insertAtHead(head, 20);
```

```
insertAtHead(head, 30);
std::cout << "Singly Linked List: ";
traverseList(head);
deleteNode(head, 20);
std::cout << "After deletion of 20: ";
traverseList(head);

// Clean up remaining nodes
while (head) {
    Node* temp = head;
    head = head->next;
    delete temp;
}
return 0;
}
```

Doubly linked lists extend the concept of singly linked lists by incorporating an additional pointer in each node. This extra pointer, often referred to as the previous pointer, allows nodes to link both to the next node and the one preceding them. Consequently, traversal in a doubly linked list can occur in both directions, which simplifies many operations such as deletion and insertion at arbitrary positions within the list. However, the added flexibility also increases the complexity of pointer manipulation, as every operation must ensure that both the next and previous pointers of the involved nodes are correctly updated to maintain list integrity.

Operations on doubly linked lists include similar actions to those found in singly linked lists—such as insertion, deletion, and traversal—but with additional considerations for maintaining backward links. For instance, when inserting a new node between two nodes, it is imperative to update the next pointer of the previous node, the previous pointer of the subsequent node, as well as the new node's own pointers. Similarly, deletion must adjust both neighboring nodes so that the chain is maintained, ensuring that there are no orphaned nodes left behind.

Although these operations can be a bit more involved, the bidirectional navigation provided by doubly linked lists is particularly useful in scenarios that require reversing the order of elements or accessing the list from both ends in an efficient manner.

A practical demonstration of a doubly linked list implementation is provided in the code snippet below. This example outlines the creation of a node structure that maintains both next and previous pointers, and includes basic functions to insert at the head, traverse the list forward, and traverse the list backward:

```cpp
#include <iostream>

// Definition for a doubly linked list node.
struct DNode {
    int data;
    DNode* next;
    DNode* prev;
};

// Insert a new node at the beginning of the doubly linked list.
void insertAtHead(DNode*& head, int value) {
    DNode* newNode = new DNode;
    newNode->data = value;
    newNode->next = head;
    newNode->prev = nullptr;
    if (head != nullptr) {
        head->prev = newNode;
    }
    head = newNode;
}

// Traverse and print the list in a forward direction.
void traverseForward(DNode* head) {
    DNode* temp = head;
    while (temp) {
        std::cout << temp->data << " <-> ";
        temp = temp->next;
    }
    std::cout << "NULL" << std::endl;
}
```

```cpp
// Traverse and print the list in a backward direction.
void traverseBackward(DNode* tail) {
    DNode* temp = tail;
    while (temp) {
        std::cout << temp->data << " <-> ";
        temp = temp->prev;
    }
    std::cout << "NULL" << std::endl;
}

int main() {
    DNode* head = nullptr;

    // Insert nodes into the doubly linked list.
    insertAtHead(head, 40);
    insertAtHead(head, 30);
    insertAtHead(head, 20);
    insertAtHead(head, 10);

    std::cout << "Doubly Linked List (Forward Traversal): ";
    traverseForward(head);

    // Move to the tail for backward traversal.
    DNode* tail = head;
    while (tail && tail->next) {
        tail = tail->next;
    }

    std::cout << "Doubly Linked List (Backward Traversal): ";
    traverseBackward(tail);

    // Clean up nodes.
    while (head) {
        DNode* temp = head;
        head = head->next;
        delete temp;
    }
    return 0;
}
```

Memory utilization in linked lists is another important consideration. In linked data structures, memory is allocated for each node individually. This dynamic allocation means that memory does not need to be contiguous, and only the memory required for the data and pointers is used. While this approach minimizes wasted space compared to static arrays allocated with a fixed size, it introduces overhead due to the storage required for pointer references. Additionally, the non-contiguous memory layout can reduce cache performance because the nodes may not be stored in neighboring memory locations. Despite these potential drawbacks, the flexibility afforded by linked lists makes them highly valuable in applications where unpredictable or frequently changing datasets are the norm.

The advantages of linked lists are evident in various practical use cases. They are particularly effective in scenarios that require frequent insertion or deletion of data, such as implementing undo features in software applications, managing a queue of tasks in an operating system, or constructing real-time data buffers. When rapid modifications to the data structure are necessary, the reallocation or shifting of elements that occurs in contiguous memory arrays can be a significant performance bottleneck. Linked data structures, by contrast, allow those modifications to occur by simply updating a few pointers, thus avoiding the need for costly memory operations.

An in-depth understanding of linked data structures is essential for effectively managing dynamic data in many computational problems. The distinction between singly and doubly linked lists extends far beyond the directional traversal of nodes; it reflects a broader consideration of the trade-offs between simplicity and flexibility. Singly linked lists offer a simple and memory-efficient means of creating linear data structures and are ideally suited for applications where data is processed sequentially from a single entry point. Doubly linked lists, with their enhanced navigational capabilities, provide additional operational convenience at the cost of increased pointer maintenance. This balance between functionality and resource usage is a recurring theme in data structure design and is critical for optimizing algorithm performance.

By integrating linked lists into broader algorithms and systems, programmers can leverage their dynamic features to design software that responds efficiently to variable data loads. Whether building a simple list for temporary data storage or constructing more complex structures such as trees that rely on nodes connected via pointers, the principles learned from linked data structures underpin much of effective software design. Their widespread use in areas such as compilers, graphical user interface development, and real-time processing systems speaks to their enduring relevance in the field of computer science.

The fundamental properties of linked data structures, including node-based storage and pointer manipulation, provide an essential framework for understanding how modern software manages memory and data. Through practical implementations, such as the provided code examples in C++, beginners can gain direct insight into the nuances of data insertion, deletion, and traversal in both singly and doubly linked lists. These operations, while conceptually simple, form the basis for more advanced topics in programming and algorithm design. The ability to dynamically manage data, update relationships among disparate nodes, and efficiently handle variations in data volume is critical for building robust and adaptable software systems.

3.4 Trees and Hierarchies

Trees are non-linear, hierarchical data structures that consist of nodes connected by edges, enabling the efficient management of complex, structured information. Unlike linear data structures such as arrays or linked lists, trees support one-to-many relationships, making them ideal for representing hierarchical relationships found in file systems, organizational charts, and various database indexing mechanisms.

At its core, a tree is composed of several fundamental components. Each node in the tree carries data and may have zero or more child nodes. The topmost node, known as the root, serves as the starting point of the tree, while nodes with no children are referred to as leaves. Intermediate nodes, which hold both a parent and one or more children, help form the branching structure of the tree. The connections between nodes are called edges, and the tree's height is determined by the length of the longest path from the root to a leaf. Other important elements include parent-child relationships, which define the hierarchical order, and siblings, which refer to nodes sharing the same parent.

Trees come in various forms, each tailored to specific requirements in data organization and retrieval. One of the simplest types is the binary tree, where every node can have at most two children, typically labeled as the left and right child. Binary trees serve as a foundation for more specialized structures such as binary search trees (BSTs) and balanced trees like AVL trees. In a binary search tree, every node's left subtree contains elements less than the node's key, while the right subtree holds elements greater than the node's key. This ordered structure provides efficient searching capabilities. AVL trees introduce additional balance constraints to maintain logarithmic height, thereby ensuring that operations such as insertion, deletion, and searching perform optimally regardless of the initial data distribution.

Focusing on binary trees, the simplicity of this structure lies in its recursive nature. Each binary tree can be seen as a root node with two subtrees that are themselves binary trees. This recursive definition lends itself well to operations like insertion and traversal. Fundamental operations on binary trees include insertion, deletion, and various forms of traversal. Traversal techniques commonly applied include inorder (left-root-right), preorder (root-left-right), and postorder (left-right-root). Inorder traversal is particularly useful in binary search trees because it visits nodes in an increasingly ordered sequence. Each traversal method carries its own time complexity considerations; typically, all these methods require visiting each node exactly once, resulting in linear time complexity, $O(n)$, where n is the number of nodes in the tree.

A concise example of a binary tree implementation in C++ illustrates these concepts. The code snippet below demonstrates how to define a binary tree node, insert nodes into the tree, and perform an inorder traversal to print the tree's elements in sorted order:

```
#include <iostream>

// Definition for a binary tree node.
struct TreeNode {
    int data;
    TreeNode* left;
    TreeNode* right;

    TreeNode(int value) : data(value), left(nullptr), right(nullptr) {}
};

// Function to insert a new node into a binary search tree.
TreeNode* insert(TreeNode* root, int value) {
```

```cpp
    if (root == nullptr) {
        return new TreeNode(value);
    }
    if (value < root->data) {
        root->left = insert(root->left, value);
    } else {
        root->right = insert(root->right, value);
    }
    return root;
}


// Inorder traversal: left subtree, root, right subtree.
void inorderTraversal(TreeNode* root) {
    if (root != nullptr) {
        inorderTraversal(root->left);
        std::cout << root->data << " ";
        inorderTraversal(root->right);
    }
}


int main() {
    TreeNode* root = nullptr;
    root = insert(root, 50);
    insert(root, 30);
    insert(root, 70);
    insert(root, 20);
    insert(root, 40);
    insert(root, 60);
    insert(root, 80);

    std::cout << "Inorder Traversal: ";
    inorderTraversal(root);
    std::cout << std::endl;

    // Memory deallocation would occur here.
    return 0;
}
```

This sample code defines a binary tree where each node is instantiated with a given value, and nodes are subsequently inserted to maintain the binary search tree property. The inorder traversal function is implemented recursively, visiting and printing nodes in order. This example emphasizes the practical mechanisms through which trees can be built and traversed efficiently.

Binary search trees take advantage of the ordered structure inherent in many applications. By ensuring that each node's left subtree contains only values less than the node's key and the right subtree only values greater, binary search trees enable efficient searching. In balanced trees, such as AVL trees, additional balancing rotations are performed during insertion and deletion to guarantee that the height of the tree remains logarithmic relative to the number of nodes, ensuring that search operations run in $O(\log n)$ time in the average and worst cases.

The layered structure of trees makes them well-suited for hierarchical data management. File systems, for example, are commonly structured as trees where directories and subdirectories form branches and files serve as leaves. Similarly, organizational charts use a tree representation to model the relationships between management and staff. In both contexts, the hierarchical nature facilitates clear, logical structuring of data, allowing for efficient navigation and retrieval.

Tree traversal techniques are crucial to extracting useful information from hierarchical structures. Depth-first search (DFS) methods such as preorder, inorder, and postorder traversals explore as far down a branch as possible before backtracking, making them ideal for tasks such as evaluating expressions or searching for a particular node. Breadth-first search (BFS), on the other hand, examines nodes level by level from the root outward, which is especially useful when the focus is on finding the shortest path in an unweighted graph or tree. Each traversal approach has its implications for performance and application suitability, and the choice among them is guided by the specific problem requirements.

Real-world applications of trees extend well beyond simple data organization. Trees play a pivotal role in database indexing schemes, such as B-trees and red-black trees, where balanced tree structures ensure rapid data retrieval. Expression parsing in compilers also relies on tree structures, with abstract syntax trees representing the nested relationships of program components. Additionally, network routing algorithms leverage trees to manage and optimize the flow of data between interconnected nodes. In each of these scenarios, the hierarchical, non-linear nature of trees contributes significantly to the efficiency and scalability of data management and access.

The operation of insertion in a tree involves comparing a new element with existing nodes and determining the correct position based on the tree's ordering rules. Deletion, on the other hand, can be more complex, especially in binary search trees where a node with two children requires finding an appropriate replacement to maintain structural integrity. Traversal and search operations are fundamental to working with trees, as they provide mechanisms for accessing and manipulating the data stored within. The performance of these operations is heavily dependent on the tree's balance; a skewed tree, which resembles a linked list, will have poor performance compared to a well-balanced tree that optimally distributes its nodes.

Hierarchical data management using trees is not confined solely to computer science theory but has practical implications in everyday applications. In a file system, for instance, the tree structure enables rapid access to files through a series of directory lookups, each of which narrows the search space. Organizational charts leverage tree structures to visualize reporting lines and departmental structures, while in web applications, the Document Object Model (DOM) of an HTML page is represented as a tree, facilitating dynamic manipulation of page elements via scripting languages.

The benefits of tree structures are underscored by their versatility and efficiency in managing complex data relationships. Their ability to represent hierarchical relationships makes them indispensable in applications where data is nested or layered. Moreover, trees enable performance optimizations through balanced structures that maintain efficient search, insertion, and deletion operations. Through proper management of these operations using traversal techniques and balancing algorithms, trees can achieve a level of performance that is essential for modern application demands.

The detailed examination of trees and hierarchies reveals that these structures are integral to the organization and efficient management of complex hierarchical data. The components of a tree, including nodes, edges, roots, leaves, and the relationships among them, form the foundation for a wide array of tree types, with binary trees being among the most widely used due to their simplicity and flexibility. Operations such as insertion, deletion, and traversal are central to exploiting the full potential of tree structures, while applications in hierarchical data management underscore their practical benefits.

By exploring tree traversal techniques—from depth-first to breadth-first—and their real-world applications in domains like database indexing and network routing, one gains an appreciation for the robustness and adaptability of tree structures. The example of a binary tree implementation provided in the code snippet serves as an accessible illustration of these concepts, demonstrating how to construct and traverse a tree efficiently. Overall, trees and hierarchies represent a powerful paradigm in data management, central to both theoretical computer science and practical application development.

3.5 Graph Structures

Graphs are mathematical structures used to model networks and relationships between entities. They consist of a set of vertices, also known as nodes, and a set of edges that connect pairs of vertices. Graphs are exceptionally versatile, capable of representing a wide variety of real-world systems such as transportation networks, social media connections, and communication grids. Their inherent flexibility makes them a powerful tool for modeling both symmetrical and asymmetrical relationships, as well as complex network behaviors.

Graphs can be classified in several ways. One primary classification distinguishes between directed and undirected graphs. In a directed graph, edges have a direction, indicating a one-way relationship between vertices, whereas undirected graphs depict bidirectional relationships, where the connection between vertices is mutual. Graphs may also be characterized as weighted or unweighted. Weighted graphs assign a cost or value to each edge, which is particularly useful in scenarios such as routing and optimization, where the weight may represent distance, time, or capacity. In contrast, unweighted graphs treat every edge equally, focusing solely on the existence of a connection rather than its magnitude. Furthermore, graphs can be cyclic, meaning they contain at least one loop or cycle, or acyclic, where no such loops exist. These classifications allow graph theory to be tailored to diverse applications, ensuring that the chosen model aligns with the specific characteristics of the problem domain.

The representation of graphs in computer memory is a critical aspect of their practical use. Two commonly employed methods are the adjacency matrix and the adjacency list. An adjacency matrix is a two-dimensional array in which rows and columns represent vertices, and each cell indicates the presence or absence of an edge between the corresponding vertices. This method is particularly useful for dense graphs where many edges are present, as it provides constant-time, $O(1)$, access to check the existence of an edge. However, for sparse graphs where the number of edges is significantly lower than the maximum possible, the adjacency matrix can consume a large amount of memory unnecessarily.

An example of an adjacency matrix is shown in Table 3.1. This table represents a simple graph with four vertices. A value of 1 indicates the presence of an edge between two vertices, while a value of 0 indicates no direct connection.

	V1	V2	V3	V4
V1	0	1	0	1
V2	1	0	1	0
V3	0	1	0	1
V4	1	0	1	0

Table 3.1: *Adjacency Matrix Representation of a Graph with 4 Vertices*

An alternative to the adjacency matrix is the adjacency list, which provides a more space-efficient representation of sparse graphs. In an adjacency list, each vertex has an associated list of the vertices to which it is connected. This method only stores edges that actually exist in the graph, thereby significantly reducing memory usage when the graph does not have many edges relative to the number of vertices. The adjacency list is especially advantageous in modeling real-world networks where connections are relatively few compared to the possible number of edges.

Graph traversal is a fundamental concept in the study and application of graph structures. Traversal algorithms are designed to explore the nodes and edges of a graph in a systematic manner, enabling the discovery of important properties such as connectivity, cycle detection, and shortest paths. Two of the most widely used traversal algorithms are Depth-First Search (DFS) and Breadth-First Search (BFS).

Depth-First Search (DFS) is a traversal technique that explores as far as possible along a branch before backtracking. DFS leverages recursion (or an explicit stack) to dive deep into the graph, visiting child nodes exhaustively prior to visiting sibling nodes. This approach is particularly effective for tasks such as detecting cycles in a graph, solving puzzles like mazes, or exploring hierarchical structures where a complete path is more informative than a shallow, broad exploration. The recursive nature of DFS means that it can be succinctly implemented, offering clear insights into the recursive structure of the graph.

A simple implementation of DFS in Python is provided in the code snippet below. This code traverses a graph represented as an adjacency list, starting from an initial vertex and marking each visited vertex to avoid infinite loops in cyclic graphs.

```python
def dfs(graph, start, visited=None):
    if visited is None:
        visited = set()
    visited.add(start)
    print(start, end=" ")

    for neighbor in graph[start]:
        if neighbor not in visited:
            dfs(graph, neighbor, visited)

# Example graph represented as an adjacency list
graph = {
    'A': ['B', 'C'],
    'B': ['A', 'D', 'E'],
    'C': ['A', 'F'],
    'D': ['B'],
```

```
    'E': ['B', 'F'],
    'F': ['C', 'E']
}

print("DFS Traversal Starting from Vertex A:")
dfs(graph, 'A')
print()
```

Breadth-First Search (BFS) employs a different strategy. Rather than delving deep into a single branch, BFS explores all neighbors of the current vertex before proceeding to the next level. This level-by-level exploration makes BFS invaluable for finding the shortest path in unweighted graphs, as it effectively examines all vertices at a given distance from the starting point before moving further away. BFS typically utilizes a queue to manage the vertices that are pending exploration, ensuring that vertices are processed in the order they are discovered.

The following Python code snippet illustrates a BFS implementation for traversing a graph. In this example, the graph is represented as an adjacency list. A queue is used to manage the order of visitation, and a set keeps track of visited vertices to prevent repeated processing.

```
from collections import deque

def bfs(graph, start):
    visited = set()
    queue = deque([start])

    while queue:
        vertex = queue.popleft()
        if vertex not in visited:
            visited.add(vertex)
            print(vertex, end=" ")
            for neighbor in graph[vertex]:
                if neighbor not in visited:
                    queue.append(neighbor)
```

```
# Example graph represented as an adjacency list
graph = {
    'A': ['B', 'C'],
    'B': ['A', 'D', 'E'],
    'C': ['A', 'F'],
    'D': ['B'],
    'E': ['B', 'F'],
    'F': ['C', 'E']
}

print("BFS Traversal Starting from Vertex A:")
bfs(graph, 'A')
print()
```

The practical applications of graph structures extend across many fields. In social network analysis, graphs are used to model relationships between users, enabling the identification of communities, influential individuals, or information flow pathways. In computer networking, graphs represent the topology of interconnected devices, guiding the design of efficient routing protocols to optimize data transfer. Graphs also play a critical role in biological networks, where they can model relationships between proteins, genes, or species, contributing to the understanding of complex biological processes. Additionally, search engines use graph-based algorithms to rank websites, while urban planning utilizes graphs to design transportation networks.

Graph representations and traversal algorithms provide the backbone for many advanced computational techniques. The use of an adjacency matrix allows for quick determination of edge existence, which is an advantage in dense graphs, while the adjacency list offers space efficiency for sparser graphs. DFS and BFS cater to different problem domains, with DFS excelling in exhaustive search and scenario analysis, and BFS providing optimal solutions for shortest-path and level-based problems. The choice of representation and traversal strategy is guided by the structure of the graph and the specific requirements of the task at hand.

The versatility of graph structures stems from their ability to model arbitrary relationships. Whether the graph represents a highly inter-connected social network, a sparse map of city roads, or a complex hierarchy of internet users, the core principles remain the same. The abstraction of vertices and edges provides a unified language for de-scribing relationships that might otherwise appear disparate across dif-ferent fields. This universality is what makes graphs one of the most important and widely studied structures in computer science and dis-crete mathematics.

As technology evolves and the scale of data continues to grow, the effi-cient representation and traversal of graphs become ever more critical. Modern algorithms often rely on the principles of graph theory to pro-cess large-scale networks in real-time. Problems such as recommen-dation systems, fraud detection, and dynamic route optimization are inherently graph-based and require both efficient memory represen-tation and rapid traversal techniques. The ongoing research in graph algorithms seeks to optimize these processes further, addressing chal-lenges posed by massive data sets that span millions of vertices and edges.

Graph structures offer a robust framework for representing networks and solving related computational problems. They provide a system-atic means of modeling complex relationships through vertices and edges, and their various classifications allow for flexibility in address-ing diverse real-world scenarios. Whether through the compact stor-age of an adjacency list or the immediate edge lookup of an adjacency matrix, the representation of graphs is integral to efficient algorithm design. Traversal methods such as DFS and BFS enable the exploration of these structures, with each algorithm offering unique benefits tailored to specific applications. The code examples provided demonstrate basic implementations of these traversal techniques, serving as a foundation for further exploration into graph theory. Overall, the study of graph structures is indispensable in the modern landscape of data analysis, network design, and algorithm development, underscoring their importance in both theoretical research and practical applications.

4

Algorithm Design Techniques

This chapter explores various strategies utilized in designing effective algorithms, focusing on approaches that enhance problem-solving capabilities. It introduces backtracking as a method for finding solutions to constraint satisfaction problems through systematic exploration of possibilities. The chapter explains greedy algorithms, highlighting their use of local optimization to achieve a global solution efficiently. Additionally, the divide and conquer technique is examined, which breaks problems into smaller subproblems that are easier to solve individually. Lastly, dynamic programming is discussed as a powerful approach for solving complex problems by breaking them down into simpler overlapping subproblems and storing their solutions for efficiency.

4.1   Backtracking

Backtracking is a systematic method for solving problems that can be framed as constraint satisfaction problems. It is a recursive, depth-first search technique in which possible solutions are incrementally built by exploring candidate choices. If at any stage the candidate does not satisfy the problem constraints, the algorithm abandons the current path and backtracks to try other alternatives. This approach is particularly useful in environments where the search space is combinatorially large, yet constraints can be used to effectively limit the number of paths explored.

At its core, backtracking operates by making a sequence of choices that gradually build a potential solution. The process involves recursively trying all possible candidates for components of the solution. When a selected candidate leads to a violation of the constraints, it is removed from the current partial solution, and another candidate is considered. The systematic exploration is similar to searching through a tree, where each node corresponds to a partial solution, and the leaves represent potential complete solutions. The recursive nature of the algorithm ensures that every possibility is explored unless it can be pruned early, which significantly reduces unnecessary computation.

The components of backtracking consist of three fundamental parts: the choice, the constraint, and the goal. The choice represents the set of available candidates that can be added to the current partial solution. Each choice must be validated against the constraints, which are rules or conditions that the solution must satisfy. Lastly, the goal is a condition that indicates that a complete solution has been constructed. A well-defined backtracking algorithm clearly specifies these three ingredients, ensuring that the algorithm can explore the solution space systematically and efficiently.

Backtracking is well-suited for problems where all possible configurations need to be tested to identify valid solutions. Notable examples include the N-Queens problem, maze solving, and generating permutations, among others. In the N-Queens problem, for example, the objective is to place N queens on an N×N chessboard such that no two queens threaten each other. Similar to many constraint satisfaction problems, the choices involve placing a queen in a specific row and column, while the constraints ensure that no queen is placed in a conflicting position. By incrementally building the board configuration and backtracking when a conflict is detected, the algorithm is able to exhaustively search for all valid placements.

Consider the N-Queens problem as an illustrative example of backtracking. In this problem, the algorithm begins by placing a queen in the first row and then moves on to subsequent rows, choosing positions that do not conflict with previously positioned queens. When a row is reached where no valid position exists, the algorithm backtracks to the previous row, changes the position of that queen, and continues the search. Through this method, every possibility is explored in a systematic manner. The following pseudocode outlines the general approach for the N-Queens problem:

```
function solveNQueens(board, row):
    if row equals board.size then
        output solution
        return
    for each column in board:
        if isSafe(board, row, column) then
            board[row][column] = queen
            solveNQueens(board, row + 1)
            board[row][column] = empty  % backtrack
```

This pseudocode clearly shows the recursive nature of backtracking. The function attempts to place a queen in each column of the current row while ensuring that the placement is safe. If a safe placement is found, the algorithm proceeds recursively to the next row. When no safe placement exists, the algorithm undoes the last move (backtracks) and tries an alternative position.

Another classic example that demonstrates the power of backtracking is the Sudoku solver. Sudoku is a puzzle that requires filling a 9×9 grid with digits so that each column, row, and 3×3 subgrid contains all digits from 1 to 9. The algorithm works by attempting to place a digit in an empty cell and then recursively solving the remainder of the puzzle. When a digit placement leads to a violation of Sudoku rules, the algorithm retracts the placement (backtracks) and attempts a different digit. The following code snippet provides a simple implementation of a Sudoku solver using the backtracking technique:

```
def is_valid(board, row, col, num):
    # Check if num is not in current row, column and 3x3 subgrid.
    for i in range(9):
        if board[row][i] == num or board[i][col] == num:
            return False
    start_row = row - row % 3
    start_col = col - col % 3
    for i in range(3):
        for j in range(3):
            if board[start_row + i][start_col + j] == num:
                return False
    return True

def solve_sudoku(board):
    for row in range(9):
        for col in range(9):
            if board[row][col] == 0:  # 0 denotes an empty cell
                for num in range(1, 10):
                    if is_valid(board, row, col, num):
                        board[row][col] = num
                        if solve_sudoku(board):
```

```
                        return True
                board[row][col] = 0  # backtrack
            return False
    return True

# Example board (0 represents empty cells)
sudoku_board = [
    [5, 3, 0, 0, 7, 0, 0, 0, 0],
    [6, 0, 0, 1, 9, 5, 0, 0, 0],
    [0, 9, 8, 0, 0, 0, 0, 6, 0],
    [8, 0, 0, 0, 6, 0, 0, 0, 3],
    [4, 0, 0, 8, 0, 3, 0, 0, 1],
    [7, 0, 0, 0, 2, 0, 0, 0, 6],
    [0, 6, 0, 0, 0, 0, 2, 8, 0],
    [0, 0, 0, 4, 1, 9, 0, 0, 5],
    [0, 0, 0, 0, 8, 0, 0, 7, 9]
]
if solve_sudoku(sudoku_board):
    print("Sudoku solved successfully!")
else:
    print("No solution exists!")
```

This Python implementation uses a helper function to check the validity of placing a number in a specific cell. The solver then recursively fills each empty cell with a valid number, backtracking when no sequential number fits. This example demonstrates how backtracking enables the algorithm to progressively construct the solution while dynamically handling constraints.

Backtracking algorithms are particularly sensitive to the size of the input and the depth of recursion. As the input size increases, the number of potential candidate solutions can grow exponentially. This situation often results in high time complexity, and in practice, heavy recursion can lead to increased memory usage and potential stack overflow errors if not managed properly. Analyzing the performance of a backtracking solution involves understanding the branching factor of the decision tree and the depth to which the algorithm must search. Optimizing performance often requires incorporating additional strategies, such as constraint propagation, that reduce the effective search space.

One way to improve the efficiency of backtracking is through pruning techniques. By analyzing the constraints at every decision point, the algorithm can discard large subsets of potential solutions that are guaranteed to lead to dead ends. Such pruning is especially beneficial when the problem domain contains many redundant or invalid configurations. For instance, in the N-Queens problem, the algorithm can eliminate entire rows or diagonals from further consideration if a queen is already placed in a conflicting position. This method not only reduces the number of recursive calls but also accelerates the convergence towards a solution.

When comparing backtracking with other algorithmic approaches such as greedy algorithms and dynamic programming, each has its strengths and limitations. Greedy algorithms make the optimum local choice at each step without reconsidering previous decisions, which can be very efficient but does not guarantee an optimal overall solution in every case. On the other hand, dynamic programming is effective when the problem exhibits overlapping subproblems and an optimal solution can be built from optimal solutions of the subproblems. Backtracking, however, is most effective in scenarios where a complete search of possibilities is required and when constraints are complex enough to prune infeasible solutions rapidly. This intrinsic flexibility makes backtracking a preferred approach for solving many combinatorial and constraint satisfaction problems.

The versatility of the backtracking paradigm lies in its ability to explore potential solutions in a structured manner while allowing modifications when a mistake is encountered. This strategy has proven successful in various domains, from solving puzzles to scheduling and beyond. As the exploration proceeds, the algorithm retains only those candidates that conform to the constraints, thereby ensuring that infeasible paths are not pursued indefinitely. This methodical exploration, when combined with intelligent heuristics for pruning the search space, results in robust solutions even for computationally challenging problems.

The systematic nature of backtracking makes it a foundational technique in algorithm design. It provides a clear framework for approaching problems where the answer is not immediately obvious but can be composed incrementally through a series of logical decisions. By breaking down complex problem structures into manageable decisions, backtracking serves as a bridge between brute force search and more elaborate algorithmic paradigms. The method's ability to retreat from incorrect paths and explore alternatives ensures that all potential solutions are considered, albeit with a focus on efficiency and practicality in well-constrained problem domains.

The backtracking method is characterized by its thorough exploration of solution spaces, enabling developers to design algorithms that are both flexible and reliable in their application. Its combinatorial nature allows for seamless iterative refinement of solutions, making it an ideal choice for solving puzzles with strict constraints and problems in operational research where all feasible configurations must be evaluated. This precision in exploration, coupled with robust techniques to prune infeasible branches, underscores the power and adaptability of backtracking methods in modern algorithm design.

4.2 Greedy Algorithms

Greedy algorithms are a class of techniques that make locally optimal choices at each step with the intention of finding a globally optimal solution. In these algorithms, decisions are made based solely on the information available at the current moment, without considering the broader implications of that decision on future choices. This approach is structured around the idea that by taking the best immediate option, one can gradually build up a complete and efficient solution to a problem.

A central concept in greedy algorithms is the greedy choice property. This property dictates that at each point in the computation, the optimal local decision will lead to an overall optimal solution. That is, the algorithm selects the option that seems best at that moment, hoping this sequence of local optimizations will accumulate to a global optimum. The hallmark of a problem suitable for a greedy strategy is that its structure must allow this property to hold; otherwise, the solution found may be suboptimal.

Underlying the effectiveness of greedy algorithms is the principle of optimal substructure. This means that an optimal solution to a problem can be constructed from optimal solutions to its subproblems. When a problem exhibits optimal substructure, solving each component optimally ensures that the overall solution is optimized. Greedy methods work particularly well on problems with this characteristic because the decision made at one step does not interfere with the decisions made at subsequent steps. In such cases, a series of local choices can be pieced together to form a complete, globally optimal answer.

There are several common characteristics that are frequently observed in greedy algorithms. First, they tend to be simple and straightforward. The decision-making process at each step is typically uncomplicated, relying on a clear evaluation criterion such as the least cost, the highest profit, or the smallest weight. Second, greedy algorithms are generally efficient in terms of time complexity, especially when compared to exhaustive search approaches. Their efficiency arises from the fact that they do not need to explore every possible solution. However, as the method involves making irreversible decisions based on local information, there exist scenarios where the greedy approach may not arrive at the global optimum. Such limitations become evident in problems where the local optimal choice does not lead to the overall best solution, highlighting the necessity for alternative strategies.

A number of problems display structures that are particularly amenable to greedy algorithm techniques. For example, Huffman coding uses a greedy approach to construct an efficient prefix code based on the frequency of symbols. Similarly, the activity selection problem, which involves scheduling the maximum number of non-overlapping activities, is classically solved using a greedy method. The algorithm for this problem selects the activity that finishes earliest, thereby freeing up resources for subsequent activities. Likewise, when constructing a minimum spanning tree (MST) for a graph, greedy strategies such as Prim's and Kruskal's algorithms are commonly employed. These algorithms seek to connect all vertices in a graph with the least total edge weight by building the spanning tree in successive steps where each new edge is chosen based on minimal cost.

In the activity selection problem, the goal is to choose the maximum number of activities that do not overlap in time. The problem is traditionally solved by first sorting the activities by their finishing times.

Once sorted, the algorithm iteratively selects the next activity that starts after the current activity finishes. The following pseudocode demonstrates how a greedy approach can efficiently select a maximal set of non-overlapping activities:

```
function selectActivities(activities):
    sort activities by finish time
    selected = []
    currentFinishTime = 0
    for activity in activities:
        if activity.start >= currentFinishTime:
            selected.append(activity)
            currentFinishTime = activity.finish
    return selected
```

This pseudocode clearly captures the greedy strategy: by continually choosing the activity with the smallest finishing time that does not conflict with the previously selected ones, the algorithm ensures that the maximum number of activities is scheduled. The selection is based entirely on local optimization—the earliest finish time is chosen without having to reconsider past selections.

Another classic application of greedy strategies is in graph theory, particularly in constructing minimum spanning trees (MSTs). Algorithms like Prim's use a greedy approach by starting with an arbitrary vertex and expanding the MST one edge at a time. At each step, the algorithm chooses the smallest weight edge that connects a vertex in the growing MST to a vertex outside of it. The following code snippet demonstrates a simple implementation of Prim's algorithm in Python:

```
import heapq

def prim_mst(graph):
    # graph is represented as an adjacency list where each key is a
    vertex
    # and the value is a list of tuples (neighbor, weight)
    start_vertex = next(iter(graph))
```

114

```python
    visited = set([start_vertex])
    edges = [(weight, start_vertex, to) for to, weight in graph[
    start_vertex]]
    heapq.heapify(edges)
    mst = []

    while edges and len(visited) < len(graph):
        weight, frm, to = heapq.heappop(edges)
        if to not in visited:
            visited.add(to)
            mst.append((frm, to, weight))
            for to_next, weight in graph[to]:
                if to_next not in visited:
                    heapq.heappush(edges, (weight, to, to_next))
    return mst

# Example usage:
graph = {
    'A': [('B', 3), ('D', 1)],
    'B': [('A', 3), ('D', 3), ('C', 1)],
    'C': [('B', 1), ('D', 1), ('E', 5)],
    'D': [('A', 1), ('B', 3), ('C', 1), ('E', 6)],
    'E': [('C', 5), ('D', 6)]
}
mst_edges = prim_mst(graph)
print("Edges in the Minimum Spanning Tree:")
for edge in mst_edges:
    print(edge)
```

In this implementation, Prim's algorithm constructs the spanning tree by always choosing the edge with the smallest weight that connects a new vertex to the tree. The process employs a priority queue (using a heap) to ensure the smallest edge is retrieved quickly. This code snippet highlights how the greedy strategy is applied in a graph-based problem, with every selection based on immediate, local optimization criteria.

Analyzing the efficiency of greedy algorithms reveals several advantages. Their straightforward approach typically leads to lower time complexities compared to exhaustive methods. For instance, the activity selection problem can be solved in $O(n \log n)$ time primarily due to the initial sorting step, while the selection process runs in linear time. When applied to graph problems such as MST construction, algorithms like Prim's can operate in $O(m \log n)$ time when implemented with a binary heap, where m represents the number of edges and n is the number of vertices. This efficiency makes greedy algorithms an appealing option for many optimization problems where resources and time are limited.

However, it is important to recognize the limitations inherent in greedy approaches. Greedy methods do not always guarantee a global optimum. Their reliance on making locally optimal choices can lead to suboptimal solutions if the problem does not strictly adhere to the greedy choice property and optimal substructure. Problems such as the 0/1 knapsack problem demonstrate this limitation; a greedy approach that selects items based on the best value-to-weight ratio may fail to produce the best overall solution. In cases where the local optimum does not naturally extend to a global optimum, alternative methods such as dynamic programming, which explores multiple combinations of choices through memoization or tabulation, can provide more accurate results.

Additionally, the performance of greedy algorithms is highly dependent on the nature of the input data and the specific constraints of the problem. The efficiency gains achieved through local optimizations can be offset in scenarios where the problem structure causes the greedy heuristic to repeatedly make non-optimal choices. In such instances, the potential exists for the solution space to be navigated in a manner that misses key combinations, thus emphasizing the importance of understanding the underlying problem properties before

116

opting for a greedy strategy.

Despite these limitations, greedy algorithms continue to be a fundamental tool in algorithm design, particularly because of their simplicity and efficiency in a wide range of applications. Their utility is not only evident in classical optimization problems but also in modern applications such as network routing, resource allocation, and even in some machine learning algorithms where quick, iterative improvements are required. Engineers and computer scientists often resort to greedy techniques as a first attempt when dealing with optimization problems, using them to generate a baseline solution that can later be compared with more complex methods.

Ultimately, the role of greedy algorithms in problem-solving is both logical and practical. Their design encourages a focus on local improvement and rapid convergence to a solution, which is especially valuable in scenarios where time constraints prohibit exhaustive searches of complex solution spaces. The balance between the benefits of immediate optimization and the occasional need for correction or backtracking underscores the need for careful consideration when applying greedy algorithms. Understanding when and why a greedy approach will yield an optimal solution is key to leveraging its strengths effectively.

The discussion of greedy algorithms illustrates both the theoretical foundations and the practical implementations of local optimization strategies. By grasping the greedy choice property and the conditions under which optimal substructure is present, one gains insight into the types of problems well-suited for greedy techniques. Whether it is through solving the activity selection problem or constructing a minimum spanning tree, greedy algorithms offer a robust framework for addressing complex issues efficiently. Their analytical simplicity, when appropriately applied, remains a cornerstone in the development of efficient algorithmic solutions, paving the way for further exploration and refinement in the vast field of computational optimization.

4.3   Divide & Conquer

Divide and Conquer is a powerful algorithm design paradigm that systematically breaks a complex problem into smaller, more manageable subproblems, solves each of these subproblems independently, and then combines their solutions to form the solution of the original problem. The core idea is to decompose a challenging problem into similar subproblems that can be addressed with simpler, often recursive, techniques, and finally to merge or combine the results to produce the overall answer. This method is widely applicable in various domains and is especially effective when the structure of the problem allows for an efficient division that significantly reduces the complexity of the problem at hand.

The approach is structured around three fundamental steps: dividing the problem, conquering each subproblem, and combining the solutions. In the first step, the original problem is split into several subproblems that are similar in nature to the original problem but smaller in size. This partitioning process is critical because it lays the groundwork for a recursive strategy, enabling the algorithm to work on a scale that is simpler and more direct than the original challenge. Once the problem is divided, the next step, the conquer phase, involves solving each of the subproblems independently. This is typically achieved using recursive techniques, where each subproblem is attacked with the same method as the original, until the subproblems become simple enough to be solved directly. Finally, in the combine phase, the solutions to the subproblems are merged in such a way that the overall solution to the original problem is constructed. This merging process must be done efficiently, as it is the key to maintaining the overall effectiveness of the divide and conquer strategy.

The division step is crucial to the overall method. During this phase, the problem is divided into smaller subproblems that closely resemble the structure of the original task. The division should be done in a way that the subproblems are not only easier to handle but also do not overlap unnecessarily. The efficiency gained here depends on the choice of how the problem is split, as poor division may lead to overlapping tasks or redundant calculations. Well-known algorithms, such as merge sort or binary search, exemplify the importance of an effective division strategy by partitioning inputs into halves or other fractional parts. In each case, the fundamental challenge is reduced into a form that is significantly simpler, and with each recursive call, the scale of the problem diminishes until a base condition is achieved.

Once the problem has been divided, the conquer phase takes over to independently solve each subproblem. This phase typically utilizes recursion, where each subproblem is handled using the same algorithmic process, ensuring that the overall method remains consistent and effective. Recursion is at the heart of the divide and conquer technique; each recursive call works on a smaller problem until a trivial base case is encountered that can be solved directly without further division. In many scenarios, these base cases are problems of size one or zero, where the solution is immediately apparent. The power of this step lies in its ability to reduce a seemingly insurmountable problem into a series of small, achievable tasks, enabling a focused approach that isolates the most challenging aspects of the original problem.

After each subproblem has been conquered through recursive resolution or direct solution, it is necessary to combine these individual solutions to derive the final answer. The combination step is often where the real ingenuity of a divide and conquer algorithm is demonstrated. It requires a careful merging of the solutions such that the aggregate result faithfully represents the solution to the overall problem. In some algorithms, this is as simple as concatenating sorted lists or merging two halves of an array, while in others, like certain geometric algorithms, it might involve more complex data structure manipulations. The efficiency of the merge step is as critical as the division and conquering phases because any inefficiencies or errors in merging can undermine the benefits accrued from dividing the problem in the first place.

Divide and conquer techniques are ideally suited to a variety of algorithmic challenges. Classic examples include sorting algorithms such as merge sort and quick sort, as well as search algorithms like binary search. Merge sort, in particular, serves as a canonical example of divide and conquer. In merge sort, the unsorted array is divided into two halves, each half is sorted recursively, and finally, the sorted halves are merged to produce a fully sorted array. The algorithm's success lies in its ability to break down the sorting process into smaller, more manageable tasks, yielding an overall performance that is both robust and efficient.

The process of merge sort begins by checking whether the array has one or no elements, in which case it is already sorted by definition. If the array contains more than one element, it is split into two roughly equal halves. Each half is then subjected to the same process of division and recursive sorting until each subarray is trivially sorted. The subsequent merging step consolidates the sorted arrays by comparing the elements of each array one by one and arranging them into a new sorted array. The pseudocode for merge sort encapsulates this process succinctly:

```
function mergeSort(array):
    if length(array) <= 1 then
        return array
    mid = floor(length(array) / 2)
    left = mergeSort(array[0:mid])
    right = mergeSort(array[mid:length(array)])
    return merge(left, right)
```

This pseudocode demonstrates the elegance of divide and conquer: it recursively divides the array until base cases are reached, then combines the results from each subarray in a manner that yields the fully sorted array. The merge function is critical here, as it must efficiently combine two sorted sequences into a single sorted sequence—a task that is done in linear time proportional to the total number of elements.

Quick sort is another highly efficient algorithm that leverages divide and conquer through a slightly different strategy. Instead of dividing an array into two equal-sized groups, quick sort selects a pivot element around which the array is partitioned. Elements less than the pivot are moved to one side, while those greater than the pivot are moved to the opposite side. This partitioning process ensures that the pivot is placed in its final sorted position. Quick sort then recursively applies the same logic to the partitions on either side of the pivot. The success of quick sort is highly dependent on the choice of the pivot, as an optimal pivot leads to balanced partitions and, thus, overall efficiency. Understanding the mechanics of partitioning is essential; the pivot selection directly impacts the number of recursive calls and the depth of recursion.

The partitioning in quick sort rearranges the elements so that all values less than the pivot precede it, and all values greater follow it. This rearrangement is typically achieved by maintaining two pointers that move towards each other from the ends of the array until they identify elements that are misplaced relative to the pivot. Once such elements are found, they are swapped, ensuring that the left side continues to contain values less than the pivot and the right side values greater. This process continues until the pointers converge, at which point the pivot is located in its rightful sorted order, and the process can be recursively applied to both halves of the array.

Solving problems with divide and conquer also requires an analysis of the algorithm's efficiency. The time complexity is commonly analyzed using recurrence relations, where the overall time is expressed in terms of the time to solve the subproblems plus the time to merge the results. For merge sort, the recurrence relation is $T(n) = 2T(n/2) + O(n)$, which resolves to $O(n \log n)$ time complexity, indicating a high degree of efficiency for sorting tasks. In quick sort, the worst-case time complexity can deteriorate to $O(n^2)$ in the case of poor pivot choices; however, with a good pivot selection strategy, the average-case complexity is $O(n \log n)$, making it a competitive option in practice.

The versatility of the divide and conquer paradigm extends to many other problems beyond sorting and searching. Binary search, for instance, exemplifies divide and conquer by reducing the search space in a sorted array with each recursive call. At every step, the algorithm compares the target value to the middle element of the array and then discards the half in which the target cannot lie, thereby rapidly converging on the target. This method scales logarithmically with the input size, making it highly efficient for large datasets.

The power of divide and conquer lies not only in solving problems but also in facilitating algorithm analysis and design. By breaking problems into their constituent subproblems, developers can better understand the structure of complex challenges and devise targeted solutions for each component. The modular nature of this approach means that improvements or optimizations in one part of the process— whether in the way the problem is divided, how the subproblems are solved, or the method used to merge the results—can directly contribute to overall performance gains. This systematic decomposition also aids in debugging and verifying correctness, as each subproblem solution can be individually validated before integrating it into the final answer.

In practice, the divide and conquer technique often serves as a building block for more advanced algorithmic strategies. It is deeply intertwined with other paradigms, such as dynamic programming, where overlapping subproblems are solved once and stored for future reference. Although dynamic programming is sometimes distinguished from pure divide and conquer by its emphasis on memoization, both approaches share the central idea of decomposing problems into simpler subcomponents. By understanding the core principles of divide and conquer, one develops a robust framework for tackling a diverse array of computational problems, spanning from numerical computations to complex data structure operations.

The challenge of combining the subproblem solutions effectively cannot be overstated. In many algorithms, merging is the step that dictates the overall efficiency. Whether it involves merging sorted lists, reconstructing tree structures, or integrating partial solutions from distributed systems, the combination step must be carefully designed to ensure that the integration does not become a performance bottleneck. A well-executed merge function leverages the structure of the subproblem solutions, ensuring that the final solution is obtained in the most efficient manner possible.

Divide and conquer remains a cornerstone strategy for solving complex problems efficiently. Its strength lies in its simplicity and generality—able to break virtually any complicated problem into parts that are simpler to understand and solve. This inherent modularity makes it an indispensable tool not only in theoretical computer science but also in practical software development. Whether sorting data, searching through large datasets, or even addressing real-world problems in fields such as image processing and computational geometry, the divide and conquer approach continues to drive innovations and improvements within the realm of algorithm design.

4.4 Dynamic Programming

Dynamic programming is a method for solving complex computational problems by breaking them down into simpler, overlapping subproblems. This technique is particularly useful when a problem can be divided such that the same subproblems are solved multiple times. Through dynamic programming, these redundant computations are avoided by storing the results of subproblems, ensuring that each subproblem is solved once and then reused when needed. The method exploits two key principles—overlapping subproblems and optimal substructure—thereby offering a systematic approach to optimizing algorithms in terms of both time and computational resources.

The principle of overlapping subproblems occurs when a recursive algorithm revisits the same problem repeatedly. Instead of recalculating the answer each time a subproblem arises, dynamic programming caches the results. This caching, commonly known as memoization, allows the algorithm to check whether the solution to a subproblem is already available before performing any further computation. By eliminating redundant calculations, the overall performance is significantly enhanced, especially in problems with exponential brute-force solutions.

Optimal substructure is the second fundamental principle of dynamic programming. It implies that the optimal solution to a problem can be constructed from the optimal solutions of its subproblems. This property ensures that, once the optimal solutions to the smaller parts of the problem have been determined, these solutions can be combined in a way that yields an optimal solution for the entire problem. When both overlapping subproblems and optimal substructure are present, dynamic programming becomes an effective strategy for computing optimal solutions efficiently.

Memoization is the top-down approach in dynamic programming. It involves writing the recursive algorithm in a natural way, but using a data structure, such as a dictionary or array, to store the results of subproblems as they are computed. Before computing a new subproblem, the algorithm first checks if the result is already stored in the cache. If it is, the algorithm reuses that value, thereby avoiding unnecessary work. Below is an example of a memoized Fibonacci function in Python, which efficiently computes Fibonacci numbers by caching the results of previous calculations:

```python
def fibonacci_memo(n, memo={}):
    if n in memo:
        return memo[n]
    if n <= 1:
        return n
    memo[n] = fibonacci_memo(n-1, memo) + fibonacci_memo(n-2, memo)
    return memo[n]
```

```
# Example usage:
print(fibonacci_memo(10))  # Output: 55
```

In this example, the function `fibonacci_memo` recursively computes the Fibonacci number for a given n. The dictionary `memo` stores previously computed Fibonacci numbers so that when the same subproblem arises, the solution is available immediately without further recursion. This top-down dynamic programming approach, achieved through memoization, optimizes recursive algorithms by preventing the re-computation of identical subproblems.

In contrast to memoization, tabulation represents a bottom-up approach to dynamic programming. With tabulation, the problem is solved by first tackling the smallest subproblems, progressively building up a table that stores these computed values. The algorithm then uses these values to solve larger and larger subproblems until the final solution is derived. This iterative method does not require recursion and therefore avoids the potential problems associated with deep recursive calls, such as stack overflow. The following code snippet demonstrates the tabulation approach for computing Fibonacci numbers:

```
def fibonacci_tab(n):
    if n <= 1:
        return n
    table = [0] * (n + 1)
    table[0] = 0
    table[1] = 1
    for i in range(2, n + 1):
        table[i] = table[i - 1] + table[i - 2]
    return table[n]

# Example usage:
print(fibonacci_tab(10))  # Output: 55
```

126

In the `fibonacci_tab` function, a list called `table` is initialized to store computed values from 0 up to n. The loop fills in the table iteratively by summing elements that represent previously calculated Fibonacci numbers. This bottom-up processing not only provides efficiency but also tends to be easier to reason about since it eliminates the need for recursion.

Dynamic programming is applied in a wide variety of problems beyond classical examples like the Fibonacci sequence. Notable applications include the Knapsack problem, coin change problems, sequence alignment in bioinformatics, and many optimization and scheduling problems. In the Knapsack problem, for instance, dynamic programming is used to determine the most valuable combination of items that can fit within a fixed weight capacity. Similarly, in coin change problems, the goal is to determine the minimum number of coins required to make a given amount, which can be efficiently computed using dynamic programming. These problems exhibit both overlapping subproblems and optimal substructure, making them ideal candidates for dynamic programming approaches.

Efficiency analysis of dynamic programming algorithms typically involves examining both time and space complexity. With memoization, time complexity is greatly improved over a naive recursive solution because each unique subproblem is computed only once. However, the storage of intermediate results increases the space complexity, which can become significant if the number of subproblems is very large. In contrast, tabulation often uses iterative loops that are more space-efficient than recursive memoization but still require a table large enough to store all intermediate solutions. Analyzing these trade-offs is essential in ensuring that a dynamic programming solution is both efficient and feasible for the problem at hand.

127

Despite its advantages, dynamic programming does come with potential drawbacks. A major challenge lies in the increased memory usage required to store the results of all subproblems. For problems with a vast number of subproblems, this can lead to significant memory overhead. Additionally, formulating a dynamic programming solution often requires a deep understanding of the problem's structure to correctly identify the overlapping subproblems and optimal substructure. This can result in complex implementations that are more difficult to design, understand, and debug, especially for beginners. Moreover, dynamic programming solutions may not always be the most efficient in every context, particularly if the problem does not strictly exhibit overlapping subproblems.

The strengths of dynamic programming lie in its ability to transform exponential time complexity problems into ones that are solvable in polynomial time through careful reuse of computed subresults. This transformation is achieved by the systematic breakdown of a problem and efficient recombination of its parts. Both memoization and tabulation have their individual advantages: memoization is conceptually simple and aligns naturally with recursive solution strategies, while tabulation provides a clear, iterative framework that can be easier to manage and debug in certain contexts. Practitioners of dynamic programming must decide between these two strategies based on the specific requirements of the problem, the constraints of the computing environment, and the clarity of the resulting code.

Dynamic programming has become an indispensable tool in algorithm design and analysis. Its power is best appreciated through problems where the same subproblems are encountered multiple times and where the optimal solution to the overall problem is built from the optimal solutions of its parts. The method's systematic structure enables the decomposition of daunting computational challenges into smaller, tractable segments, each contributing to the final solution. Whether using memoization to capture the results of recursive calls or leveraging tabulation to construct solutions iteratively, dynamic programming offers a flexible and robust framework for optimizing complex problems.

Integrating dynamic programming techniques into algorithmic problem-solving not only improves efficiency but also deepens one's understanding of the problem's inherent structure. The process encourages a methodical approach where dependencies between subproblems are assessed and efficiently managed. This discipline encapsulated within dynamic programming enhances both the design and the scalability of algorithms, making it an essential strategy in software development, especially in areas requiring optimal solutions under resource constraints.

Through dynamic programming, complex algorithms become more manageable as each subcomponent is systematically addressed and stored for future use. This leads to significant improvements in computational performance, particularly in problems where the number of potential inputs or decision points grows rapidly. While dynamic programming may introduce additional memory overhead, its practical benefits in terms of reducing computational time make it one of the most powerful techniques in the algorithmic toolbox.

The strategic choice of dynamic programming, whether through memoization or tabulation, extends far beyond academic exercises. In real-world applications, it is routinely used in fields such as operations research, economics, and bioinformatics, where the efficient resolution of complex, multidimensional problems is critical. As software systems grow in complexity and the demand for fast, reliable solutions increases, dynamic programming continues to play a vital role in the development of efficient and scalable algorithms.

4.5 Advanced Heuristic Techniques

Heuristic techniques are algorithmic approaches that aim to find satisfactory, "good-enough" solutions for complex problems when exact methods become computationally prohibitive. These methods trade off optimality for speed and efficiency, making them particularly valuable in scenarios where exact solutions require excessive time or resources. Heuristics are characterized by their simplicity, speed of execution, and the ability to deliver feasible solutions under constraints of limited computing power, even if these solutions are not guaranteed to be optimal.

Fundamentally, heuristics are designed to quickly traverse large solution spaces and to provide practical answers in situations where an exhaustive search is impossible due to the combinatorial nature of the problem. The primary characteristics of heuristic techniques include their speed, simplicity, and flexibility. They are built to operate under constraints, making them extremely useful when the problem size is large or when a real-time response is required. However, this efficiency comes with the trade-off that the solutions obtained may not be the absolute best possible; rather, they are acceptable approximations that satisfy the overall objectives of the problem.

There are several types of heuristic techniques, each with its unique approach and applicability. Among these, greedy heuristics represent one of the simplest forms, making locally optimal choices at every step in pursuit of a global solution. Greedy methods are straightforward; they select the best immediate option without backtracking, thus re-

ducing the computation time. While these methods are computationally efficient and easy to implement, they can sometimes fall into local
optima, resulting in solutions that are not globally optimal.

Local search techniques take a different approach by starting with an
initial solution and iteratively improving it by exploring its neighbor-
hood. The idea is to refine an existing solution through small, incremental changes, continuously seeking to enhance the quality of the
solution. Local search is particularly effective in optimization scenarios where the solution space is too large to permit an exhaustive evaluation. A practical example of local search is the hill climbing algorithm, which examines neighboring solutions and moves in the direction that improves the objective function. A simple code example in
Python demonstrates this concept by attempting to maximize a function through iterative improvement:

```python
import random

def objective_function(x):
    # Example: a simple quadratic function with maximum at x = 5
    return -(x - 5) ** 2 + 25

def hill_climbing(max_iterations=100, step_size=0.1):
    # Start with a random initial solution between 0 and 10
    current_solution = random.uniform(0, 10)
    current_value = objective_function(current_solution)

    for _ in range(max_iterations):
        # Create a candidate solution in the neighborhood
        candidate_solution = current_solution + random.uniform(-step_size
, step_size)
        candidate_value = objective_function(candidate_solution)

        # Move to the candidate solution if it improves the value
        if candidate_value > current_value:
            current_solution = candidate_solution
            current_value = candidate_value

    return current_solution, current_value
```

```
solution, value = hill_climbing()
print("Optimized Solution:", solution)
print("Objective Function Value:", value)
```

This code illustrates a local search optimization by starting with a random value and iteratively refining it to maximize an objective function. The hill climbing method implemented here demonstrates how local modifications can effectively improve the solution even when a globally optimal outcome is not guaranteed.

Another category of heuristic techniques is inspired by natural processes, with genetic algorithms being a prime example. Genetic algorithms mimic the process of natural selection by generating a population of candidate solutions and evolving them over successive iterations. In this process, solutions are evaluated based on a fitness function, and the best solutions are selected to produce offspring through operations such as crossover (combining parts of two solutions) and mutation (introducing random changes). Over time, the population converges towards better solutions. Although genetic algorithms may consume more computational resources compared to simpler heuristics, their ability to escape local optima makes them highly effective in complex landscapes.

Simulated annealing is another notable heuristic. It is inspired by the annealing process in metallurgy, where controlled cooling of a material reduces defects, leading to a more stable structure. Similarly, simulated annealing begins with a high "temperature" that allows the algorithm to accept worse solutions with a certain probability. As the temperature decreases, the algorithm becomes more conservative, gradually focusing on improving the solution. This probabilistic acceptance of poorer solutions early on enables simulated annealing to explore the solution space more thoroughly and potentially escape local minima that might trap other heuristic methods.

Each of these heuristic approaches has distinct practical applications in a wide range of optimization problems. In real-world scenarios, heuristics are essential in scheduling, where the goal might be to minimize the total time needed for a series of tasks while managing complex constraints. For instance, in route planning, heuristics are used to quickly determine low-cost or time-efficient routes among numerous possibilities. Resource allocation in industrial operations or network resource distribution in telecommunications are additional areas where heuristics provide practical, efficient solutions.

Assessing the performance of heuristic techniques involves evaluating several metrics, including the quality of the solution and the computational speed. Since heuristics do not guarantee an optimal solution, a common approach is to compare the heuristic output with the best-known or theoretically optimal solution, if available. Computational speed is also a critical factor; often, a heuristic might be preferred if it provides a sufficiently good solution within a fraction of the time that an exact algorithm would require. In addition, the scalability of the heuristic is important, as a method that works well for small problems might encounter challenges when applied to problems of much larger size.

The performance of heuristic techniques is highly context-dependent. Greedy heuristics are most beneficial in situations where taking the best immediate action leads naturally towards a good overall solution. Yet, in more complex scenarios, such as those with multiple competing objectives or where the solution landscape contains many local optima, more sophisticated methods like genetic algorithms or simulated annealing are often preferable. Local search techniques, by iteratively refining an initial solution, have shown significant promise in handling problems where incremental improvement is feasible and beneficial. Selecting the appropriate heuristic method, therefore, requires a deep understanding of the problem characteristics, the available computational resources, and the acceptable trade-offs between solution quality and execution time.

While heuristic techniques deliver multiple benefits, they are not without limitations. The inherent trade-off in these methods is that, while they often provide acceptable solutions quickly, they do not guarantee global optimality. In some cases, the solution produced by a heuristic may be significantly suboptimal if the method gets trapped in a local optimum or if the parameters of the heuristic (such as step size in local search or cooling schedule in simulated annealing) are not well-tuned for the specific problem instance. Moreover, the stochastic nature of methods like genetic algorithms and simulated annealing means that results may vary from run to run, potentially requiring multiple executions to achieve a satisfactory solution.

Despite these challenges, the benefits of heuristic techniques are substantial, particularly in practical applications where the cost of computing an exact solution is prohibitive. Their ability to provide near-optimal solutions quickly renders them an indispensable tool in modern optimization scenarios. Industries ranging from logistics and transportation to manufacturing and telecommunications have leveraged these methods to solve large-scale, complex problems that would otherwise be intractable.

Advanced heuristic techniques continue to evolve as researchers and practitioners gain a deeper understanding of complex system behaviors. Innovations in algorithm design often involve hybrid approaches, where different heuristic methods are combined to balance their strengths and mitigate their weaknesses. For example, a genetic algorithm might be used to find a good initial solution, which is then refined using local search techniques. Such hybrid methods harness the exploratory power of global search methods and the precision of local search, resulting in solutions that are both robust and efficient.

In practical settings, the use of heuristic techniques can lead to significant cost savings and performance improvements. Consider, for instance, the application of simulated annealing in designing integrated circuits, where finding the optimal layout is crucial for performance but the design space is enormous. By applying simulated annealing, engineers can quickly converge on layouts that, while not absolutely optimal, yield substantial improvements in efficiency and power consumption relative to manually designed circuits. Similarly, in supply chain management, heuristic methods help optimize routes and schedules, leading to reductions in operational costs and improved service levels.

Evaluating the overall performance of heuristic techniques requires a balanced approach that considers both the quality of the solution and the computational resources expended. Metrics such as convergence speed, the robustness of the solution across different runs, and sensitivity to parameter tuning are all important considerations. In many cases, experimental validation through benchmarks and real-world case studies is used to assess the efficacy of a particular heuristic technique.

Advanced heuristic techniques represent a critical component of the optimization toolbox, enabling practitioners to handle complex, real-world problems that are beyond the reach of exact algorithms. Their focus on delivering good-enough solutions quickly makes them invaluable in domains where computational resources are limited or where real-time decisions are required. Although these methods do not guarantee optimal solutions, their practical effectiveness in providing satisfactory results under challenging conditions is well established. As optimization problems grow more intricate and the demands on system efficiency increase, heuristic techniques will continue to play an essential role in the development of advanced, scalable solutions.

5

Sorting and Searching Techniques

This chapter delves into fundamental algorithms used for sorting and searching data efficiently. It begins by outlining the importance of sorting, discussing various sorting techniques, such as comparison-based algorithms like bubble sort and insertion sort, alongside more advanced methods like merge sort and quick sort. The chapter also examines non-comparison sorting algorithms, including counting sort and radix sort, highlighting their unique advantages. Additionally, it explores essential searching techniques, with a focus on linear and binary search principles, illustrating how different algorithms can impact performance based on data structure and size. Ultimately, the chapter emphasizes the significance of choosing the right sorting and searching techniques for optimizing algorithm efficiency.

5.1   Fundamentals of Sorting

Sorting is defined as the process of organizing the elements of a list or an array into a particular sequence, typically in ascending or descending order. In computer science, the ability to sort data is central to many algorithms and processes. The very act of sorting takes an unsorted or arbitrarily ordered collection and transforms it into a systematically arranged structure. This ordered structure not only facilitates human comprehension when data is examined but also serves as a critical underpinning for many computational procedures that rely on the properties of ordered sequences.

Sorting plays a pivotal role in effective data organization, a fundamental aspect of computer science. By rearranging data into a coherent sequence, sorting enables rapid searches and efficient data management. For instance, when data is sorted, binary search algorithms can be applied, significantly reducing the number of comparisons required to locate a particular element compared to searching through unsorted data. This reduction in computational effort is essential when dealing with large volumes of data. In addition, sorted data optimizes various operations, such as merging datasets and performing set operations, which in turn improves overall system performance and algorithm efficiency.

The significance of sorting extends beyond algorithmic efficiency. It is directly applied in many real-world scenarios that require the organization of vast amounts of information. Database indexing relies on sorting to arrange records, allowing for expedited queries and rapid data retrieval. In environments where search speed is crucial, such as in real-time systems or large-scale e-commerce platforms, sorting

138

the underlying data improves responsiveness. In data visualization, sorted data can reveal trends, patterns, and anomalies that might otherwise remain hidden in a disordered dataset. Furthermore, sorted information contributes to spatial data organization in geographic information systems, where the physical or logical arrangement of data points is critical for accurate mapping and analysis.

Sorting techniques can be broadly divided into comparison-based and non-comparison sorting algorithms. Comparison-based algorithms, such as bubble sort, insertion sort, merge sort, and quick sort, determine the order of input elements solely by comparing them against one another. Non-comparison sorting methods leverage specific properties of the input data, such as integer values or key distributions, to achieve sorting without performing direct element-to-element comparisons. A clear understanding of these categories is essential for recognizing the intrinsic strengths and limitations inherent in each approach.

Several key characteristics influence the performance and suitability of a sorting algorithm. These include time complexity, space complexity, stability, and adaptability. Time complexity describes how the computational effort required by an algorithm increases with the size of the input, and it is typically expressed in Big O notation. Sorting algorithms may exhibit behaviors ranging from linear to quadratic, or even better performance in advanced methods. Space complexity measures the extra memory required by an algorithm, a critical factor when processing large datasets within limited memory constraints. Stability ensures that elements with equal keys maintain their relative order after sorting, which is particularly important in multi-key sorting operations. Adaptability refers to how well an algorithm can adjust its performance based on the characteristics of the input data, such as when dealing

139

with nearly sorted sequences or specific distributions.

Understanding the time complexity associated with sorting algorithms is crucial to assessing their performance in practical applications. In sorting, there are typically three scenarios to consider: best case, average case, and worst case. The best-case scenario may occur when the input data is already sorted, allowing algorithms such as insertion sort to run in linear time. Conversely, the worst-case scenario might involve completely unsorted data, causing some algorithms to degenerate to quadratic time performance. For example, bubble sort and insertion sort both have worst-case time complexities of $O(n^2)$, which makes them inefficient for large, arbitrarily ordered datasets. However, more advanced techniques like merge sort and quick sort achieve average and worst-case complexities of $O(n \log n)$, offering improved performance even under adverse conditions. Understanding these complexity bounds is crucial when selecting an appropriate sorting algorithm for a particular application.

Stability is a cornerstone concept in sorting algorithms. Stable sorting ensures that equal elements retain the same relative order as in the input sequence after the sorting process is completed. This property is vital in scenarios where multiple sorting criteria must be maintained. For instance, when sorting a list of records first by date and then by name, a stable sorting algorithm guarantees that records with identical dates remain in the correct order by name. This aspect is instrumental when the sorted output serves as input for additional processing or when maintaining historical order is necessary. Not all sorting algorithms are stable by default; for example, quick sort is typically unstable, requiring careful modification if stability is desired.

A firm grasp of basic sorting terminology is essential when discussing and comparing different methods. Common terms include "swap," which refers to the exchange of two elements within an array to move them into their correct positions; "partitioning," the process of dividing an array into subarrays around a pivot element, particularly in quick sort; and "sorting in place," which describes algorithms that rearrange elements within the original data structure without using substantial additional memory. Familiarity with these terms enhances the ability to comprehend algorithm descriptions and engage in meaningful analysis of their performance characteristics.

In contrast to comparison-based sorting, non-comparison sorting algorithms offer an alternative approach by exploiting additional properties of the elements. These methods do not rely on the relative order of pairs of elements during the sorting process. Instead, they use the inherent structure of the keys—such as integer range or digit positions—to organize data effectively. Techniques such as counting sort and radix sort can achieve impressive performance metrics, sometimes sorting in linear time relative to the number of elements, provided that the range or distribution of keys is suitably constrained. Although non-comparison sorting algorithms have specific requirements and limitations regarding the types of data they can process, they serve as powerful tools in scenarios where these constraints are met.

A detailed exploration of sorting algorithm examples broadens the understanding of various approaches. Bubble sort, for instance, repeatedly compares adjacent elements and swaps them if necessary, gradually moving the largest or smallest elements to the ends of the list. Despite its simplicity, bubble sort is known for its poor efficiency on large datasets. Insertion sort builds a sorted list incrementally by repeatedly inserting an element into its appropriate position, making it efficient for nearly sorted or small arrays. More advanced methods, such as merge sort and quick sort, utilize the divide and conquer paradigm

141

to recursively split the dataset into smaller partitions, sort them, and then merge the results. Merge sort consistently delivers stable performance with a time complexity of $O(n \log n)$ and requires additional space, while quick sort is revered for its speed and efficiency in practice, despite its worst-case potential of $O(n^2)$ under certain conditions. Such comparisons help delineate the particular advantages and trade-offs of each algorithm.

Selecting the appropriate sorting algorithm requires careful consideration of several factors, including the size of the input, the nature of the data, and system resource constraints. When working with small or nearly sorted datasets, simpler algorithms like insertion sort may offer a preferable balance between simplicity and computational overhead. In contrast, large datasets with no inherent order often necessitate more sophisticated approaches, such as quick sort or merge sort, to ensure acceptable performance. Input characteristics, such as the range of key values or the presence of duplicate entries, can also influence algorithm choice—especially when stability is a concern or when specific data distributions render non-comparison sorting methods more advantageous. Environmental constraints, such as available memory and processing power, further dictate the selection of one algorithm over another. These considerations highlight the importance of tailoring algorithm selection to the problem at hand, ensuring that the chosen method aligns with both performance requirements and practical limitations.

A comprehensive understanding of the fundamentals of sorting involves synthesizing knowledge of definitions, importance, applications, and the various algorithmic approaches available. Sorting is not merely a theoretical exercise but a practical tool that underpins many operations in data management and computation. By organizing data effectively, sorting improves the efficiency of other algorithms, enables swift information retrieval, and supports complex operations such as multi-dimensional data analysis. Grasping the diverse characteristics of sorting algorithms—from basic terminology to advanced properties like stability and time complexity—equips practitioners with the analytical tools necessary to evaluate and choose the most appropriate algorithm for a given context.

5.2   Comparison-Based Sorting

Comparison-based sorting is a method where the order of elements in a list or array is determined by direct comparisons between individual elements. This technique forms the foundation for many popular sorting algorithms, as it relies on determining whether one element should precede another based on some comparison criterion. Its fundamental nature makes it a reliable and widely studied approach in computer science, particularly when handling data types for which a natural ordering exists.

One of the strengths of comparison-based sorting algorithms is their broad applicability. These algorithms are designed to work with any data elements that can be compared using a binary relation, such as numbers, characters, or even structured objects with defined comparison operations. Their versatility ensures that they are used in many common applications—from sorting names in a directory to ordering complex records in a database. This prevalence and reliability make comparison-based sorting an integral part of algorithm education and practical application in software development.

Among the comparison-based techniques, bubble sort and insertion

143

sort are two of the most fundamental algorithms taught to beginners. Bubble sort is known for its simplicity and ease of understanding, albeit at the cost of efficiency for larger data sets. The algorithm repeatedly iterates through the list, comparing pairs of adjacent elements. If the elements are out of order, they are swapped, effectively "bubbling" the largest (or smallest) elements to the end of the list over successive passes. This process continues until no swaps are needed in an entire pass through the list, signalling that the array has achieved a sorted order. Despite its straightforward approach, bubble sort exhibits a quadratic time complexity in the worst case, making it less suitable for sorting large arrays.

The iterative process of bubble sort can be described through a series of clear steps. Initially, the algorithm starts at the beginning of the list and compares the first element with the second. If the first is larger than the second in the case of ascending order, the two elements are swapped. The algorithm then moves to the next pair, continuing this comparison and swap process until the end of the list is reached. With each full pass through the list, the largest unsorted element is moved to its correct position at the end. The process is repeated on the remaining unsorted portion of the list until no further swaps are required, indicating that the entire list is sorted.

```
def bubble_sort(arr):
    n = len(arr)
    # Loop through all elements in the array
    for i in range(n):
        swapped = False
        # Last i elements are already sorted
        for j in range(0, n - i - 1):
            # Compare adjacent elements
            if arr[j] > arr[j + 1]:
                # Swap if they are in the wrong order
                arr[j], arr[j + 1] = arr[j + 1], arr[j]
                swapped = True
```

```
        # If no two elements were swapped by inner loop, break
        if not swapped:
            break
    return arr

# Example usage
unsorted_list = [64, 34, 25, 12, 22, 11, 90]
sorted_list = bubble_sort(unsorted_list)
print(sorted_list)
```

This code demonstrates the bubble sort technique applied to an array of integers. Each pass through the list effectively pushes the highest remaining element to its correct end position. However, because each element may require multiple comparisons and swaps, bubble sort's worst-case performance is $O(n^2)$. This quadratic growth in runtime is the main drawback of bubble sort when applied to large or random data sets, as the number of comparisons and swaps increases rapidly with the size of the list.

Inserting into a sorted sequence is another foundational idea in comparison-based sorting, and insertion sort is a prime example of this approach. Insertion sort builds a sorted array gradually, starting from the leftmost element and inserting each new element into its correct position within the already sorted portion. It accomplishes this by comparing the new element with the elements of the sorted subarray, shifting these elements one position to the right until the correct insertion point is found. This approach results in a sorted array as the algorithm processes each element sequentially.

The iterative procedure within insertion sort is intuitive and straightforward. The algorithm begins by assuming that the first element is already sorted. It then takes the second element and compares it with the first, inserting it into the appropriate position to maintain the sorted order. For every subsequent element, the algorithm compares it with

145

elements in the sorted subarray from right to left, shifting elements as necessary to make room for the insertion of the new element. This process is repeated until every element has been inserted into its correct sorted position, resulting in a fully ordered list.

```python
def insertion_sort(arr):
    # Traverse through 1 to len(arr)
    for i in range(1, len(arr)):
        key = arr[i]
        j = i - 1
        # Move elements of arr[0..i-1], that are greater than key,
        # to one position ahead of their current position
        while j >= 0 and key < arr[j]:
            arr[j + 1] = arr[j]
            j -= 1
        arr[j + 1] = key
    return arr

# Example usage
unsorted_list = [12, 11, 13, 5, 6]
sorted_list = insertion_sort(unsorted_list)
print(sorted_list)
```

The code snippet above provides an example of insertion sort implemented in Python. The algorithm works by iterating from the second element to the end of the list, using a key to store the value of the element to be inserted. As the algorithm traverses backward through the sorted portion, it shifts elements until it finds the right location for the key. The resulting sorted list is output after the process is complete. In scenarios where the data is nearly sorted or the array size is small, insertion sort can operate in linear time, $O(n)$, making it a highly efficient algorithm under these conditions. However, in the worst-case scenario, where the data is in reverse order, the time complexity again reaches $O(n^2)$.

The comparative analysis of bubble sort and insertion sort provides valuable insights into the trade-offs between simplicity and efficiency in comparison-based sorting methods. Both algorithms are straightforward in concept and implementation, making them excellent educational tools for understanding core sorting principles. Bubble sort is often considered less efficient due to its repeated passes and redundant comparisons, especially when the array is significantly unsorted. Insertion sort, by contrast, takes advantage of the partially sorted structure as it builds its sorted subarray, which can lead to superior performance on nearly ordered datasets. Furthermore, while insertion sort generally requires fewer operations than bubble sort in such cases, its nested loop structure can still lead to quadratic behavior in worst-case scenarios.

When comparing the two, ease of implementation is a key factor. Bubble sort is conceptually simpler because it relies on adjacent comparisons and swaps. However, it is inefficient in practice due to the large number of necessary comparisons even when the list is nearly sorted. Insertion sort may involve more complex inner loop logic to manage the shifting of elements, but this additional complexity translates to more efficient handling of data that is already partially sorted. In real-world applications, these characteristics guide the decision on which algorithm to use. For example, insertion sort is often preferred in situations where the dataset is small or nearly sorted, while bubble sort is mainly of academic interest or used in cases where algorithmic simplicity is paramount.

Despite the limitations in performance, both bubble sort and insertion sort play a critical role as introductory sorting algorithms. They illustrate key concepts such as iterative processing, conditional swapping, and element shifting, which form the basis for understanding more complex sorting techniques. The study of these algorithms helps elucidate the importance of time complexity and efficiency considerations when scaling algorithms to handle larger data sets. Additionally, these methods provide a solid conceptual framework that lays the groundwork for learning advanced algorithms like merge sort and quick sort, which use divide and conquer strategies to achieve better performance characteristics.

In practical terms, the iterative nature of bubble sort involves making multiple passes over the data, with each pass ensuring that the largest unsorted element reaches its proper position in the final sorted list. While the simplicity of bubble sort makes it easy to understand and implement, its efficiency issues serve as an important caution in algorithm design: even clear, logically correct methods may exhibit suboptimal performance characteristics if not carefully optimized for the specific problem context. In contrast, insertion sort's strategy of inserting elements into an already sorted portion of the array emphasizes the optimization potential inherent in algorithms that exploit existing order. This approach demonstrates that slight changes in methodology can lead to substantial improvements in performance, particularly in cases where the input data exhibits favorable characteristics.

The teaching value of these algorithms extends beyond their immediate use in sorting operations. Studying the differences between bubble sort and insertion sort helps students and novice programmers understand how algorithm design choices impact computational complexity. Detailed examination of the iterative steps and conditions under which each algorithm operates provides insights into the broader principles of algorithm analysis. For instance, the best-case scenario for insertion sort, when the data is almost sorted, offers a clear example of how algorithm performance can improve dramatically with minor variations in input order. Similarly, the inefficiency of bubble sort under the same

148

conditions reinforces the necessity of selecting algorithms that are well-suited to the problem's constraints.

Overall, comparison-based sorting algorithms such as bubble sort and insertion sort serve as essential tools in the educator's toolkit. They not only introduce fundamental techniques of comparison and swap operations but also illustrate vital concepts about performance trade-offs and algorithmic efficiency. By studying these algorithms, learners develop a deeper understanding of the critical role that design decisions play in algorithm implementation, especially in contexts where performance influences the overall capability of a software system. The insights gained from analyzing these algorithms continue to inform the development of more advanced sorting techniques, broadening the scope of algorithm design and refinement in the field of computer science.

5.3   Divide & Conquer Sorting

Divide and conquer sorting is a strategy that addresses the complexity of sorting by decomposing the overall problem into smaller, more manageable subproblems. The core concept is to split a large dataset into pieces, sort each piece independently, and then combine the sorted pieces in an efficient manner. This approach is inherently recursive: the problem is continuously divided until it becomes trivial to solve, and the solutions to these subproblems are then merged to form a complete, sorted result.

The importance of the divide and conquer strategy lies in its ability to handle large datasets efficiently. By reducing a complex problem into smaller components, the sorting process can take advantage of parallel processing and optimized recursive algorithms. This method is particularly effective for sorting as it minimizes the number of comparisons and movements needed overall. The ability to break down the problem and combine results systematically allows algorithms such as merge sort and quick sort to outperform simpler methods on large collections of data.

Merge sort exemplifies the divide and conquer strategy through its recursive structure and systematic merging process. Merge sort begins by dividing the original list into two roughly equal halves. Each half is then recursively split into smaller subarrays until the arrays consist of a single element, which by definition is already sorted. Once these small arrays are obtained, the algorithm begins the process of merging: two sorted subarrays are combined by comparing their elements and placing the smaller element first in a new array. This merging process is repeated as the subarrays are combined back to the original size, ultimately producing a completely sorted list.

The essential steps of merge sort involve an initial division phase followed by a merging phase. During the division phase, the algorithm splits the list into two halves, recursively invoking the sort on each half. In the merging phase, a dedicated function takes two sorted arrays as input and produces a single sorted array. This merge function compares the elements at the start of each subarray and sequentially builds the final result by inserting the smaller element until one subarray is exhausted; the remaining elements from the other subarray are then appended to the resulting array.

```
def merge(left, right):
    merged = []
    i = j = 0
    while i < len(left) and j < len(right):
        if left[i] <= right[j]:
```

150

```
            merged.append(left[i])
            i += 1
        else:
            merged.append(right[j])
            j += 1
    merged.extend(left[i:])
    merged.extend(right[j:])
    return merged

def merge_sort(arr):
    if len(arr) <= 1:
        return arr
    mid = len(arr) // 2
    left = merge_sort(arr[:mid])
    right = merge_sort(arr[mid:])
    return merge(left, right)

unsorted_list = [38, 27, 43, 3, 9, 82, 10]
sorted_list = merge_sort(unsorted_list)
print(sorted_list)
```

In the code above, the function `merge_sort` recursively breaks down the list into subarrays until they are simple enough to be directly merged, while the `merge` function is responsible for efficiently combining two sorted arrays. The merge function works by using two pointers to track the current element of each subarray and comparing the elements step-by-step to build the final sorted array. This precise merging procedure is what gives merge sort its overall stability and efficiency.

The time complexity of merge sort is consistently $O(n \log n)$, regardless of the initial ordering of the data. The reason for this efficiency is twofold. First, the division phase logarithmically reduces the size of the problem by repeatedly splitting the list in half, which contributes a factor of $\log n$. Second, the merging phase requires a linear traversal of each subarray, resulting in a factor of n. When these two factors are combined, the overall time complexity remains $O(n \log n)$ in both the average and worst-case scenarios. This predictable performance makes merge sort particularly suitable for systems where worst-case guarantees are crucial.

Quick sort is another divide and conquer sorting algorithm that uses a pivot-based partitioning strategy to achieve efficient sorting. In quick sort, the algorithm selects a pivot element from the list and then partitions the remaining elements into two subarrays: one consisting of elements less than or equal to the pivot and the other containing the elements greater than the pivot. Unlike merge sort, which divides the list into two equal halves regardless of the data distribution, quick sort's division is based on the pivot, which ideally results in balanced subarrays for efficient recursion.

The partitioning process in quick sort is central to its operation. During partitioning, the algorithm scans the array and maintains two regions— one for elements that are less than the pivot and another for those that are greater. Common implementations use pointers that move from the beginning and end of the array towards each other, swapping elements that are on the wrong side of the pivot. Once the pointers meet, the pivot is placed in its correct position in the array, ensuring that all elements to its left are less than or equal to it and all elements to its right are greater. This partitioning step is the key that allows the recursive sorting of the divided subarrays.

```
def partition(arr, low, high):
    pivot = arr[high]
    i = low - 1
    for j in range(low, high):
        if arr[j] <= pivot:
            i += 1
            arr[i], arr[j] = arr[j], arr[i]
    arr[i + 1], arr[high] = arr[high], arr[i + 1]
    return i + 1

def quick_sort(arr, low, high):
```

```
    if low < high:
        pi = partition(arr, low, high)
        quick_sort(arr, low, pi - 1)
        quick_sort(arr, pi + 1, high)
    return arr

unsorted_list = [10, 7, 8, 9, 1, 5]
sorted_list = quick_sort(unsorted_list, 0, len(unsorted_list) - 1)
print(sorted_list)
```

In this implementation, the partition function rearranges the array by placing all elements smaller than the pivot before it and those greater than the pivot after it. This ensures that the pivot is in its final sorted position. The quick_sort function then recursively calls itself on each partition, thereby sorting the entire array. It is important to note that while quick sort generally offers superior performance on average, its worst-case time complexity can degrade to $O(n^2)$ if the pivot selection is poor—typically when the smallest or largest element is consistently chosen as the pivot. However, with effective pivot selection, such as using the median-of-three method, quick sort can maintain an average-case complexity of $O(n \log n)$.

The analysis of quick sort's time complexity underscores the critical role of pivot selection. In the ideal scenario, the pivot divides the array into two nearly equal halves, leading to a logarithmic recursive depth combined with linear work at each level of recursion. This results in the average-case time complexity of $O(n \log n)$. Nevertheless, in pathological cases where the data is already sorted or nearly sorted, and if the worst-case pivot is repeatedly chosen, the algorithm's performance can degrade significantly. In practical applications, however, careful pivot selection strategies and hybrid approaches that switch to simpler algorithms for small subarrays mitigate these issues, making quick sort one of the most widely used sorting algorithms in practice.

The merits of divide and conquer strategies in sorting are evident when comparing the performance, efficiency, and scalability of merge sort and quick sort. Both algorithms leverage the idea of breaking down the problem into subproblems that are easier to handle, but they approach the merging and partitioning differently. Merge sort guarantees stable O(n log n) performance regardless of the initial dataset, which is particularly valuable in scenarios where predictability is important. Quick sort, on the other hand, often outperforms merge sort in practical applications due to lower constant factors and better cache performance, provided that the pivot is chosen well. This balance of theoretical robustness and practical efficiency makes divide and conquer sorting strategies essential tools in the programmer's arsenal.

The divide and conquer methodology offers a powerful framework for developing efficient sorting algorithms. Merge sort and quick sort, as two prominent examples, demonstrate how recursive decomposition combined with efficient merging or partitioning can lead to significant improvements in sorting performance. The systematic breakdown of a complex problem into simpler parts, followed by the careful recombination of these parts, allows large datasets to be sorted in a time-efficient manner. Such strategies not only improve computational efficiency but also provide clear pathways for further algorithmic optimization and adaptation to various data characteristics.

5.4   Non-Comparison Sorting

Non-comparison sorting refers to a class of algorithms that sort data by relying on properties inherent in the input elements rather than by directly comparing pairs of elements. These algorithms capitalize on specific characteristics of the data, such as the range of integers or the structure of digits in numbers, to determine order with methods that are distinct from the traditional pairwise comparison approach. This method of sorting is particularly beneficial in situations where the data fits characteristics that allow for linear or near-linear performance, outperforming comparison-based algorithms whose lower bound is generally $O(n \log n)$.

The importance of non-comparison sorting becomes evident when dealing with data types for which the input values fall within a known range or exhibit a uniform structure. In scenarios involving integers, characters, or fixed-length strings, non-comparison methods can leverage the predictability of these data types to achieve more efficient sorting. For instance, when sorting a large collection of numbers where the maximum value is not significantly greater than the number of elements, non-comparison sorts like counting sort can execute in linear time relative to the number of elements plus the range of input values. This performance advantage makes them suitable for applications such as processing large datasets in databases, sorting user IDs, or organizing log records.

Counting sort is a classic example of a non-comparison algorithm that sorts elements by counting the number of occurrences of each distinct input value. The algorithm begins by iterating over the input array and tallying the frequency of each unique element into a counting array. This array is then transformed into a cumulative count array, which effectively maps each input value to its final position in the sorted output. Once the cumulative counts are established, the algorithm places each element from the original array into its correct position in a new output array. Counting sort assumes that the input consists of non-negative integers and that the range of input values (denoted as k) is not signif-

155

icantly larger than the number of items to be sorted. Its simplicity and efficiency make it particularly attractive for specific applications where these conditions are met.

Counting sort operates in a straightforward manner. Initially, an auxiliary array is created to hold counts of each individual element present in the input data. Following this, the algorithm processes the count array to compute cumulative counts, which indicate the final sorted positions of the elements. Finally, starting from the end of the original array to maintain stability, it places each element into its appropriate location in the sorted output using the cumulative count array and decrements the count accordingly. The overall time complexity of counting sort is $O(n + k)$, where n is the number of elements in the input and k is the range of the input values. This linear time complexity is particularly advantageous when k is not excessively larger than n.

```
def counting_sort(arr):
    if not arr:
        return arr
    # Determine the range of input values.
    k = max(arr)
    # Initialize the counting array with zeros.
    counts = [0] * (k + 1)
    # Count each occurrence in the input array.
    for num in arr:
        counts[num] += 1
    # Compute cumulative counts.
    for i in range(1, len(counts)):
        counts[i] += counts[i - 1]
    # Initialize the output array.
    output = [0] * len(arr)
    # Place each element in its correct position.
    for num in reversed(arr):
        output[counts[num] - 1] = num
        counts[num] -= 1
    return output

# Example usage
unsorted_list = [4, 2, 2, 8, 3, 3, 1]
```

```
sorted_list = counting_sort(unsorted_list)
print(sorted_list)
```

The above code clearly demonstrates the counting sort algorithm in action. By counting the frequency of each element and then computing a cumulative frequency, the algorithm is able to determine the precise location for each element in the final sorted array. The sorted output is produced with stability, meaning that the relative order of elements with equal values is preserved.

Radix sort is another non-comparison algorithm that leverages the individual digits of numbers to perform sorting. Instead of comparing whole numbers, radix sort processes each number digit by digit, typically starting from the least significant digit (LSD) and working its way up to the most significant digit (MSD). This two-phase sorting process involves a stable sorting algorithm, like counting sort, to sort the numbers based on each individual digit. The stable sort ensures that the ordering of digits sorted in previous passes remains intact as new digit levels are processed. Consequently, after each pass, the partially sorted array becomes closer to being fully sorted, until the entire array is ordered correctly.

The operation of radix sort can be broken down into clear phases. First, the algorithm determines the maximum number of digits present in any number within the input array. Then, for each digit position starting from the least significant digit, counting sort is applied to sort the array according to that digit. Because counting sort is stable, the relative order of numbers sorted in previous iterations is maintained. This iterative process continues until all digit positions have been processed, resulting in a fully sorted array. The efficiency of radix sort is influenced by both the number of elements and the number of digits in the largest element, typically expressed as $O(d \cdot (n + k))$, where d is the digit length, n is the number of elements, and k is the range of the digit values (often 10 for decimal numbers).

```
def counting_sort_for_radix(arr, exp):
    n = len(arr)
    output = [0] * n
    counts = [0] * 10
    # Count occurrences of digits
    for num in arr:
        index = (num // exp) % 10
        counts[index] += 1
    # Compute cumulative count
    for i in range(1, 10):
        counts[i] += counts[i - 1]
    # Build the output array in a stable manner
    for num in reversed(arr):
        index = (num // exp) % 10
        output[counts[index] - 1] = num
        counts[index] -= 1
    return output

def radix_sort(arr):
    # Find the maximum value to determine the number of digits.
    max_val = max(arr)
    exp = 1
    while max_val // exp > 0:
        arr = counting_sort_for_radix(arr, exp)
        exp *= 10
    return arr

# Example usage
unsorted_list = [170, 45, 75, 90, 802, 24, 2, 66]
sorted_list = radix_sort(unsorted_list)
print(sorted_list)
```

In the radix sort implementation, the helper function counting_sort_for_radix is specialized to process one digit at a time by considering the exponent value exp. For each digit position, a stable sort is enforced using counting sort, ensuring the relative order is maintained for digits that have already been processed.

This sequential digit processing eventually produces a completely sorted array, demonstrating how non-comparison methods can effectively sort data based on their numeric representation.

The time complexity of radix sort is typically $O(d \cdot (n + k))$. In this expression, d represents the number of digits in the maximum number, n is the number of elements in the input array, and k is the base of the numeral system (commonly 10 for decimal systems). When d is constant or grows slowly in relation to n, radix sort can outperform comparison-based algorithms, especially for large datasets where the keys are multi-digit numbers. The use of counting sort in its inner loop ensures that radix sort remains efficient, despite the seemingly repetitive nature of processing each digit separately.

When comparing counting sort and radix sort, both algorithms are powerful tools in contexts where the structure of the data permits bypassing the lower bound of comparison sorting. Counting sort is extremely efficient when the range of input values is relatively small, as its time complexity scales linearly with n and k. However, counting sort becomes less practical as the range of data increases significantly because the size of the counting array grows correspondingly, potentially leading to inefficient use of memory.

Radix sort, on the other hand, extends the applicability of non-comparison methods to larger ranges of numbers by focusing on individual digit positions instead of the entire number at once. While radix sort uses counting sort as its subroutine, the overall performance is influenced by the number of digits in the maximum element rather than the maximum value itself. This makes radix sort well-suited for sorting large numbers or strings where the number of characters is confined within a practical limit, ensuring that it remains efficient even when the numeric range is extensive.

159

Despite their efficiencies, both counting sort and radix sort have limitations. Counting sort is inherently tied to discrete, non-negative integers and requires that the data falls within a manageable range. Radix sort, while more flexible in terms of range, still depends on the underlying stability of its sorting subroutine and is generally applied only to data that can be decomposed into constituent parts, such as digits in a number. The specific characteristics of the dataset should inform the choice between these two methods, as well as compared to traditional comparison-based sorting algorithms.

The key takeaway is that non-comparison sorting methods, particularly counting sort and radix sort, offer significant performance benefits in specialized contexts. They circumvent the inherent lower bound of $O(n \log n)$ associated with comparison-based sorting and can approach linear time performance given favorable conditions. These advantages make them valuable in performance-critical applications such as real-time data processing, high-volume transaction systems, and environments where sorting efficiency directly impacts overall throughput. By understanding the underlying mechanics and appropriate use cases, programmers can effectively leverage these algorithms to optimize system performance.

The comparative analysis of counting sort and radix sort reveals that each method has its own niche of efficiency. Counting sort is particularly appropriate when the input elements are integers within a limited range, as its simplicity and linear performance make it an attractive option. Radix sort extends this capability to more complex data types that can be broken down into digits or characters, thereby providing a flexible yet efficient alternative for large-scale sorting tasks. Choosing between these algorithms requires careful consideration of the dataset characteristics, including the range, distribution, and the representation of the input values.

In essence, non-comparison sorting algorithms provide a powerful means to achieve high-performance sorting by exploiting structural properties of the input data. These methods underscore the fundamental idea that not all sorting problems require direct comparison between elements. Instead, by tailoring an approach to the specifics of the input, one can achieve significant gains in both speed and efficiency. This insight is particularly valuable in fields where large datasets are the norm and computational resources are at a premium, reinforcing the relevance of non-comparison sorting techniques in modern computer science.

5.5   Search Techniques

Search techniques are fundamental methods used to locate a specific element or value within a data structure such as an array, list, or database. The effectiveness of these techniques is critical for designing efficient software applications, as they directly impact responsiveness and performance. Efficient searching is essential in a broad range of applications, from querying databases in real-time systems to scanning large datasets for critical information. The choice of a search algorithm can have significant performance implications, especially when handling large-scale data where even small inefficiencies become magnified.

One of the simplest search techniques is linear search. Linear search works by inspecting each element of the data structure sequentially until the target element is found or until all elements have been examined. This method is particularly intuitive because it mimics the way a person might manually look through a list: start at the beginning and check each item one by one until reaching the desired value. Its straightforward nature makes linear search an ideal introductory algorithm for beginners learning about search techniques.

The algorithm for linear search can be described in several clear steps. First, the search begins at the very first element of the data structure. The element is compared to the target value. If the current element matches the target, the search terminates successfully, returning the position of the element. If it does not match, the algorithm moves to the next element in sequence. This process continues until either the target is found or all elements have been checked. Because every element in the data structure may need to be inspected in the worst-case scenario, the time complexity of linear search is $O(n)$, where n is the number of elements in the structure. This makes linear search less efficient for large datasets, but its simplicity and minimal requirements (no need for sorted data) make it useful in specific situations.

```
def linear_search(arr, target):
    for index, value in enumerate(arr):
        if value == target:
            return index  # Return the index where the target is found
    return -1  # Return -1 if target is not present in the array

# Example usage
data = [5, 3, 7, 1, 9, 2]
target_value = 7
result = linear_search(data, target_value)
print("Index of target:", result)
```

The code snippet above demonstrates a basic implementation of linear search in Python. The function iterates over each element in the provided list, using the built-in `enumerate` function to track both the index and the value. If the target value is found, the index is immediately returned; otherwise, the function returns -1 to indicate that the target is not present. Despite its simplicity, the linear search remains an important algorithm due to its constant applicability regardless of whether the data is sorted.

For scenarios involving sorted data, a more efficient method known as binary search is widely used. Binary search takes advantage of the ordering in the dataset, significantly reducing the number of comparisons required to locate an element. The fundamental principle behind binary search is the divide and conquer strategy: by repeatedly dividing the search interval in half, the algorithm rapidly narrows down the potential location of the target element.

The process of binary search begins by comparing the target value to the element in the middle of the sorted data structure. If the target is equal to this middle element, the search is complete. If the target is less than the middle element, the algorithm discards the upper half of the data structure; conversely, if the target is greater, the lower half is discarded. This halving of the search space is repeated on the remaining subarray, eventually reducing the size of the search space to a single element. The efficiency of this approach is evident in its time complexity, which is $O(\log n)$ in both the average and worst-case scenarios. This logarithmic growth makes binary search extremely efficient for large arrays.

The algorithmic steps for binary search can be summarized as follows. Initially, two pointers (often named `low` and `high`) are set to define the current bounds of the search, with `low` indicating the beginning and `high` the end of the array. The algorithm then calculates the midpoint of this interval. If the target matches the element at the midpoint, the algorithm returns the index of the target. If the target is less than the midpoint value, the search continues in the lower half of the array by adjusting the `high` pointer; if it is greater, the `low` pointer is adjusted to narrow the search to the upper half. These steps are repeated until the target is found or the interval diminishes to zero, indicating that the target is not present.

```
def binary_search(arr, target):
    low, high = 0, len(arr) - 1
    while low <= high:
        mid = (low + high) // 2  # Find the midpoint
        if arr[mid] == target:
            return mid  # Target found, return index
        elif arr[mid] < target:
            low = mid + 1  # Continue search in the upper half
        else:
            high = mid - 1  # Continue search in the lower half
    return -1  # Target not found in the array

# Example usage
sorted_data = [1, 3, 5, 7, 9, 11, 13]
target_value = 7
result = binary_search(sorted_data, target_value)
print("Index of target:", result)
```

The above code snippet outlines a typical implementation of binary search in Python. The function begins by setting low to zero and high to the last index of the sorted list. Within a while loop, the midpoint is computed and used to compare against the target value. Depending on whether the target is less than or greater than the middle value, the algorithm adjusts the search boundaries by updating either the low or high index. This process continues until either the target is found or the search space is exhausted, in which case the function returns -1.

The performance advantages of binary search become particularly apparent when analyzing its time complexity. In a sorted array, binary search's iterative approach reduces the size of the search space by half with each step. As a result, the number of comparisons required grows logarithmically with the number of elements, leading to a time complexity of $O(\log n)$. This efficiency makes binary search overwhelmingly superior to linear search for large datasets, as the number of comparisons remains relatively modest even as n grows large. In contrast, linear search may require traversing the entirety of the dataset, resulting in a worst-case time complexity of $O(n)$.

While binary search is highly efficient, its successful application depends on the data being sorted. This precondition is crucial; otherwise, the algorithm cannot guarantee that halving the search space correctly discards non-relevant data. Due to this requirement, there are scenarios where linear search might be the preferable method. For instance, in unsorted arrays or data structures with unpredictable ordering, linear search remains the method of choice despite its higher time complexity in the worst-case scenario. Additionally, for small datasets where the overhead of sorting might not be justified, linear search can offer a simpler and more direct solution.

The trade-offs between linear search and binary search highlight essential considerations for algorithm selection in varied contexts. Linear search boasts its simplicity and ease of implementation and can be applied universally, regardless of the initial order of the data. Its robust performance on small or unsorted datasets makes it a reliable default in many practical situations. On the other hand, binary search leverages the sorted nature of data to achieve dramatically faster search times in larger datasets, with the trade-off being the prerequisite of pre-sorted input. In practice, determining which search technique to employ requires an understanding of the dataset's characteristics, including its size, ordering, and the frequency with which the data is updated or searched.

Applications of these search techniques extend across numerous fields in computer science. In database systems, for example, indexing is critical to ensure quick retrieval of records, and binary search is commonly used to navigate the indexes of large, sorted datasets. Similarly, in operating systems, file systems often rely on efficient search algorithms to quickly access files and directories. In real-time applications where responsiveness is paramount, the difference between $O(n)$ and $O(\log n)$ time complexity can directly translate to noticeable performance improvements. Even in everyday programming tasks such as filtering data in a spreadsheet or implementing search features in software applications, choosing the right search algorithm can significantly enhance the user experience.

Importantly, the study of search techniques not only involves understanding the mechanics of algorithms like linear and binary search, but also appreciating the underlying principles of algorithm efficiency and design. The development of these techniques reflects broader concepts in computer science, such as the importance of data organization, the impact of input characteristics on algorithm performance, and the interplay between algorithmic simplicity and computational complexity. By examining the detailed steps of these search methods and comparing their efficiencies, learners gain valuable insights into how algorithmic decisions affect overall system performance and scalability.

The techniques discussed here also underscore vital lessons in algorithmic optimization. In many real-world applications, the choice of search method is just one aspect of a multifaceted problem-solving approach. Factors such as memory usage, preprocessing time (for sorting in the case of binary search), and the frequency of search operations all play significant roles in determining the most appropriate algorithm. For example, in a dynamic environment where data is constantly being modified, maintaining a sorted dataset for binary search might be less practical than using linear search. Conversely, in a scenario where numerous search operations are performed on relatively static data, the initial cost of sorting the data can be greatly offset by the efficiency gains of using binary search.

Overall, both linear and binary search techniques are crucial for navigating data structures effectively. Linear search, with its simplicity and universal applicability, provides a straightforward approach that directly inspects each element regardless of the dataset's order. Binary search, although more complex in its implementation and dependent on pre-sorted data, offers superior performance for large datasets by leveraging the divide and conquer principle to reduce the search space exponentially. The decision between these two methods hinges largely on the nature of the dataset and the specific performance requirements of the application.

The systematic exploration of these search methods serves as a foundation for understanding more advanced search algorithms and data retrieval strategies. Learners gain practical insight into algorithm design and complexity analysis by comparing the $O(n)$ worst-case performance characteristic of linear search with the $O(\log n)$ efficiency offered by binary search. These comparisons not only highlight the trade-offs between simplicity and efficiency but also reinforce the importance of choosing the right algorithm based on the problem's context. The knowledge of when to apply each strategy is critical for optimizing software performance and ensuring that systems can handle data-intensive tasks effectively.

Search techniques such as linear search and binary search are indispensable tools in the realm of computer science. Each has its own strengths and limitations, and understanding these trade-offs is key to effective algorithm selection. By mastering these fundamental search methods, practitioners are better equipped to design and implement

solutions that are both efficient and robust, ensuring optimal performance in a wide range of applications.

6

Graph Algorithms

This chapter covers essential concepts related to graph structures, including vertices, edges, and the distinctions between directed and undirected graphs. It explores various graph traversal techniques, focusing on Depth-First Search (DFS) and Breadth-First Search (BFS), and their applications in navigating through graph data. The chapter also examines algorithms for finding the shortest paths in graphs, such as Dijkstra's algorithm, and techniques for constructing minimum spanning trees, including Prim's and Kruskal's algorithms. Additionally, it highlights advanced graph algorithms relevant for specific problems, such as network flows and connectivity. Overall, the chapter emphasizes the practical applications of graph algorithms in real-world scenarios like networking, logistics, and social media analysis.

6.1   Graph Fundamentals

Graphs are mathematical structures employed to model relationships between distinct objects. In its simplest form, a graph comprises a set of vertices, often referred to as nodes, and a set of edges, which are the connections between these vertices. Vertices serve to represent individual entities in a system, whether these are individuals in a social network, intersections in a transportation system, or data points in computations. Edges, on the other hand, depict the relationships or interactions between these vertices. This foundational concept provides a robust framework for analyzing complex systems in diverse fields, ranging from computer science to operations research.

The study of graphs involves a precise examination of their core components and inherent properties. At the most basic level, a graph is defined by its vertices and edges. Vertices are typically abstract elements that can be considered as points, while edges are conceptual lines linking these points. The importance of these core components lies in their ability to encapsulate a wide array of relationships. An edge connecting two vertices signifies a relation, and the characteristics of this edge can have significant implications. For instance, in a network modeling communication channels, an edge might symbolize the existence of a direct connection between two nodes, suggesting the possibility of data exchange.

Graphs can be categorized into various types according to the nature of their vertices and edges. One of the primary classifications differentiates between directed and undirected graphs. In a directed graph, commonly known as a digraph, each edge possesses an intrinsic orientation. This means that an edge from vertex A to vertex B is distinctly different from an edge directed from vertex B to vertex A. This directional property is crucial when representing scenarios such as one-way streets in transportation networks or precedence constraints in scheduling problems. In contrast, undirected graphs do not assign a direction to their edges. Instead, the connection between vertices is mutual, representing a bidirectional or symbiotic relationship. This attribute is particularly useful for modeling systems where the direction of the relationship is either irrelevant or inherently bidirectional, such as collaborations in a network of researchers.

Another important dimension in graph theory is the concept of weights on edges, which gives rise to weighted and unweighted graphs. In a weighted graph, each edge carries a numerical value that often represents cost, distance, or capacity. This scalar measure is essential in many practical applications such as transportation, logistics, and network routing, where optimizing some cost function is paramount. On the contrary, an unweighted graph treats all edges as equal, disregarding any differences in cost or capacity. Although unweighted graphs are simpler to analyze, weighted graphs provide a more nuanced representation of many situations in real-world systems.

Graph representation in computer memory is a critical concept for both theoretical analysis and practical algorithm implementation. Two common representations include adjacency matrices and adjacency lists. An adjacency matrix is a two-dimensional array used to represent relationships between vertices. In this representation, both the rows and columns correspond to the vertices in the graph. Each entry in the matrix indicates whether an edge exists between the pair of vertices corresponding to that row and column, and in the case of weighted graphs, it may also store the numeric weight associated with that edge. Consider the following example of an adjacency matrix, which demon-

171

strates how the presence or absence of edges can be systematically recorded:

	Vertex 1	Vertex 2	Vertex 3
Vertex 1	0	1	0
Vertex 2	1	0	1
Vertex 3	0	1	0

In the table above, a '1' indicates that an edge exists between the corresponding vertices, while a '0' implies no direct connection. This method is particularly advantageous when dealing with dense graphs, where the number of edges is close to the maximum number possible. However, for sparse graphs that have relatively few edges, the adjacency matrix may become inefficient in terms of memory usage.

By contrast, an adjacency list provides an alternative and often more space-efficient method for representing graphs, especially when the graph is sparse. In this representation, each vertex is associated with a list of its neighboring vertices. This means that rather than storing a complete matrix, one only records the edges that actually exist. Such representation is beneficial not only for saving memory but also for efficiently traversing graphs, as it provides direct access to the list of connected vertices for any given vertex.

Properties of graphs further enhance our understanding of their structure and utility. One significant property is the degree of a vertex, which is defined as the number of edges incident to it. In directed graphs, one may distinguish between the in-degree and out-degree of a vertex, where the in-degree is the number of edges arriving at the vertex, and the out-degree is the number of edges leaving it. Another important property is connectivity, which refers to the degree to which vertices in a graph are linked together. A connected graph is one in which there is a path between every pair of vertices, while a discon-

172

nected graph contains at least one pair of vertices for which no such path exists. In addition, the concept of bipartiteness in graphs unfolds the capability of partitioning the vertex set into two subsets, such that no two vertices within the same subset are directly connected. This property is particularly useful in problems related to matching and scheduling, where it is crucial to divide a set of entities into two groups with minimal conflict.

In directed graphs, often referred to as digraphs, the concept of established direction on each edge is paramount. Directed graphs are characterized by pairs of vertices that maintain a defined order. The existence of an edge from one vertex to another indicates a one-way relationship, which is essential in applications where order and direction play a critical role. Such scenarios include modeling dependencies in task scheduling, where the sequence of activities must be maintained, or representing hierarchies where an element influences subsequent elements. This unidirectional flow is critical in ensuring that the propagation of information or functions through a system adheres to a specified order, thereby maintaining consistency and clarity in dynamic systems.

In contrast, undirected graphs present a scenario where the existence of an edge signifies a reciprocal relationship between vertices. The lack of directionality means that if vertex A is connected to vertex B, then vertex B is inherently connected to vertex A. This mutual connection is a fundamental characteristic used in many fields, such as social network analysis, where relationships like friendship or mutual interest do not imply any unilateral dependency. The simplicity of undirected graphs makes them a popular choice in many introductory studies of graph theory because they effectively capture and communicate an inherent symmetry in interactions.

173

The nuanced distinction between weighted and unweighted graphs is instrumental in understanding the quantitative aspects of graph theory. In weighted graphs, the presence of a numerical value on an edge introduces a layer of complexity that is pivotal for optimization problems. For instance, when applied to navigation systems, the weight may represent the distance between two intersections, and the goal is to compute the shortest or most efficient route. Conversely, unweighted graphs treat all edges uniformly, which simplifies analysis but at the expense of overlooking the potential variability in the strength or cost of connections. This dichotomy not only influences the choice of algorithms used for analysis but also affects the computational complexity of the operations performed on the graph.

Graph representation techniques such as adjacency matrices and adjacency lists serve as the backbone for practical implementations of graph algorithms. The adjacency matrix, as demonstrated earlier, allows for constant-time checks to determine whether a given pair of vertices is directly connected. However, its memory requirements increase quadratically with the number of vertices, making it less suitable for graphs where the number of vertices is large and the number of edges is relatively small. Adjacency lists, while more memory efficient, necessitate the traversal of lists to find specific connections, which can influence the time complexity of certain graph algorithms. The decision on which representation to use is therefore contingent upon the structure of the graph and the demands of the specific problem at hand.

Evaluating the properties of graphs reveals much about the underlying structure of the modeled system. In undirected graphs, the degree distribution of vertices provides insights into the balance and concentration of connections, where vertices with a high degree may serve

174

as central hubs in a network. Conversely, in directed graphs, analyzing the differential between in-degrees and out-degrees can uncover sources and sinks within the network, highlighting vertices that serve as primary broadcasters or recipients of information. The connectivity of a graph is often the subject of rigorous study, as it impacts the robustness and resilience of the network. Graphs that are highly connected tend to be more resistant to random failures, which is a critical consideration in the design of networks such as power grids or communication networks.

The study of graphs extends beyond the representation of static connections; it encompasses the dynamic interactions between elements as well. As such, the properties of graphs are not only abstract mathematical considerations but also practical tools for analyzing real-world systems. For instance, determining whether a graph is bipartite can have immediate applications in scheduling and resource allocation, where it is necessary to divide a set of tasks or entities into distinct groups without overlap. Similarly, the characterization of a graph through its connectivity properties can influence the design of efficient communication protocols in distributed systems, where ensuring that every node remains reachable is paramount.

The fundamental principles discussed here provide a comprehensive overview of graph theory, outlining the essential components, types, and methods of representation that are indispensable for the analysis of networks. The clear definitions of vertices and edges, the exploration of directed versus undirected graphs, and the distinction between weighted and unweighted graphs create a solid foundation for further study in graph algorithms. The use of adjacency matrices and adjacency lists illustrates practical approaches to representing these structures in computer memory, while the examination of graph properties such as degree and connectivity underscores the relevance of these concepts in computational problems. This integrated understanding of graphs is pivotal for modeling and analyzing complex relationships in various applications, underscoring their widespread importance and utility in solving both abstract and practical problems.

6.2 Graph Traversal Techniques

Graph traversal is a fundamental method for visiting all nodes in a graph systematically. This technique is essential for numerous computational tasks, including searching, pathfinding, and gaining a deeper understanding of a graph's structure. In many practical applications, the order in which nodes are visited can significantly affect performance and the outcome of algorithms. Traversal methods enable the discovery of connected components, detection of cycles, and the establishment of shortest paths in various graph-based structures.

The significance of graph traversal lies in its ability to methodically explore the entirety of a graph. By traversing a graph, algorithms can perform a breadth of operations including the analysis of connectivity, the determination of optimal routes, and the identification of specific patterns within data. Graph traversal is central to tasks such as network routing, social network analysis, and even in solving puzzles where the structure of connections greatly influences results.

Depth-First Search (DFS) is one of the primary traversal strategies applied within graph theory. DFS is characterized by its approach of exploring as deeply as possible down one branch of the graph before backtracking and exploring alternatives. The methodology makes DFS particularly well-suited for tasks that require exhaustive exploration

of possibilities or the discovery of connected regions within a graph.
The algorithm initiates the traversal at a starting vertex, marking it as
visited, and then recursively proceeds with one of its unvisited neighboring vertices. This process of lateral deepening continues until there
are no more unvisited vertices along the current path, at which point
the algorithm backtracks to explore alternate branches.

The key steps of the DFS algorithm can be summarized as follows. Initially, a starting vertex is chosen and marked as visited. The algorithm
then inspects each adjacent vertex of this starting point. If it encounters an adjacent vertex that has not been visited, DFS recurses into that
vertex, repeating the process. Once all adjacent vertices have been explored, the algorithm backtracks to the preceding vertex, continuing
the exploration until every vertex reachable from the initial vertex has
been visited. The inherently recursive nature of DFS makes it both
straightforward in concept and powerful in its execution, especially
when implemented using a recursive programming paradigm.

A simple example of DFS implemented in a beginner-friendly programming language can illustrate this approach effectively. The following code snippet demonstrates a recursive DFS implementation in
Python:

```python
def dfs(graph, vertex, visited=None):
    if visited is None:
        visited = set()
    visited.add(vertex)
    print(vertex)  # Process the vertex (e.g., print it)
    for neighbor in graph[vertex]:
        if neighbor not in visited:
            dfs(graph, neighbor, visited)
    return visited

# Example usage:
graph = {
    'A': ['B', 'C'],
```

177

```
    'B': ['A', 'D', 'E'],
    'C': ['A', 'F'],
    'D': ['B'],
    'E': ['B', 'F'],
    'F': ['C', 'E']
}
dfs(graph, 'A')
```

In this example, the function dfs traverses each node starting from a chosen vertex, printing each vertex as it is visited. The recursive calls ensure that all vertices that are accessible from the starting point will eventually be processed, and the use of a Python set prevents the algorithm from revisiting any vertex.

The time complexity of DFS is generally $O(V + E)$, where V represents the number of vertices and E the number of edges in the graph. This efficiency arises from the fact that each vertex and edge is examined at most once during the traversal. Such computational performance is particularly advantageous for large graphs, ensuring that even extensive networks can be processed in a reasonable amount of time.

In contrast to DFS, Breadth-First Search (BFS) offers an alternative method of graph traversal that focuses on exploring nodes level by level. In BFS, the algorithm begins at a selected starting vertex and explores all the neighboring nodes at the current level before moving to the next level. This level-order traversal is performed by employing a queue to maintain the order in which vertices are visited. The algorithm enqueues the starting vertex and then proceeds to dequeue vertices, enqueuing any of their unvisited neighbors in turn. By processing vertices in the order of their distance from the starting vertex, BFS effectively measures the shortest path in unweighted graphs, making it a popular choice for pathfinding problems.

The steps involved in the BFS algorithm can be outlined as follows. The process starts with selecting a root vertex and enqueuing it. The algorithm then repeatedly dequeues a vertex, marks it as visited, and enqueues its unvisited adjacent vertices. This continues until the queue is empty, at which point every reachable vertex from the starting point has been explored. The systematic manner in which nodes are visited—by level—ensures that the first time a node is encountered, it is reached via the shortest possible path from the root vertex.

A practical implementation of BFS can also be demonstrated using a programming language such as Python. The following example provides a code snippet that highlights the iterative, queue-based structure of BFS:

```python
from collections import deque

def bfs(graph, start):
    visited = set()
    queue = deque([start])
    while queue:
        vertex = queue.popleft()
        if vertex not in visited:
            print(vertex) # Process the vertex (e.g., print it)
            visited.add(vertex)
            queue.extend(neighbor for neighbor in graph[vertex] if
    neighbor not in visited)
    return visited

# Example usage:
graph = {
    'A': ['B', 'C'],
    'B': ['A', 'D', 'E'],
    'C': ['A', 'F'],
    'D': ['B'],
    'E': ['B', 'F'],
    'F': ['C', 'E']
}
bfs(graph, 'A')
```

This implementation utilizes Python's deque from the collections module to efficiently manage the queue operations. The algorithm iterates over nodes by removing a vertex from the front of the queue, processing it, and then adding its neighbors, ensuring that the breadth-first ordering is maintained throughout the traversal.

Similar to DFS, the time complexity of BFS is $O(V + E)$, a reflection of the fact that every vertex and edge is processed in the traversal process. BFS is especially useful when the goal is to determine the shortest path from a given start node in an unweighted graph or to explore all nodes connected to the start node in a methodical sequence.

Both DFS and BFS are powerful tools within the domain of graph traversal, each possessing attributes that render them particularly suited to specific kinds of applications. Depth-First Search is widely applied in scenarios where exploring deeper connections is necessary. Its recursive structure makes it particularly effective for solving problems like maze navigation, topological sorting, and cycle detection. Additionally, DFS is instrumental in tackling complex tasks that involve backtracking and exhaustive path exploration. On the other hand, Breadth-First Search is typically preferred when the objective is to find the shortest distance between nodes or to examine the structure of a graph layer by layer. BFS is fundamental in applications such as social network analysis—where determining the shortest path between individuals can reveal influential relationships—and in network broadcasting protocols where the minimal number of hops is crucial.

The applications of DFS and BFS extend beyond academic exercises, finding roles in real-world systems. For instance, pathfinding algorithms in urban planning and transportation networks frequently rely on these traversal techniques to compute efficient routes between locations. In robotics, both DFS and BFS can be used to navigate through obstacle-laden environments as a robot attempts to map its surroundings. In addition, many algorithms in computer security utilize graph traversal methods to detect vulnerabilities, such as identifying cycles or isolated nodes in network configurations.

While both traversal techniques share a common time complexity, their practical utility often hinges on the specific requirements of the task at hand. DFS, with its exploration of a single branch before backtracking, provides a pathway to deeper insights within data structures that possess a hierarchical or nested nature. Conversely, BFS delivers comprehensive coverage of levels, ensuring that the shortest paths are recognized efficiently. The choice between DFS and BFS is further informed by additional factors such as memory usage patterns. DFS, particularly when implemented recursively, may lead to increased call stack usage, whereas BFS requires additional memory for the queue structure it employs. In many applications, these considerations must be weighed against the overarching objectives of the problem.

The integrated use of both DFS and BFS in algorithm design can result in highly robust systems. For example, many algorithms will initially use BFS to determine a preliminary ordering or to detect the presence of disconnected components and then switch to DFS for a more in-depth analysis of certain subcomponents. This combination allows for a balance between rapid, surface-level insights and detailed, recursive explorations. Moreover, hybrid techniques that blend characteristics of both DFS and BFS are sometimes developed to leverage the strengths of both methods, particularly in complex systems where dynamic changes occur or where both breadth and depth of analysis are required.

The methodology behind graph traversal encapsulates a blend of simplicity and depth. Graph traversal techniques such as DFS and BFS form a core component of the toolkit for solving numerous computational problems. Their ability to break down complex structures into manageable parts underpins many algorithms used in network analysis, resource optimization, and problem-solving. Whether the goal is to comprehend the overall structure of an extensive network or to pinpoint the shortest route in a navigation system, these traversal techniques provide the algorithmic foundation necessary for effective analysis.

An understanding of the intrinsic mechanisms and performance characteristics of DFS and BFS is indispensable for further studies in graph theory and algorithm design. As graphs become increasingly prevalent in modeling data in various fields, the importance of efficient and effective traversal methods cannot be overstated. The fundamental strategies presented here—recursive depth-first exploration and iterative breadth-first search—illustrate the critical balance between thoroughness and efficiency. This balance is central to designing algorithms that are both scalable and adaptable, capable of addressing diverse computational challenges encountered in practice.

6.3 Shortest Path and Spanning Trees

The study of shortest path algorithms and spanning trees occupies a central role in graph theory. Shortest paths refer to the minimum distance or cost route from a given source vertex to any other vertex in a graph, while spanning trees are acyclic subsets of a graph that connect all vertices with the minimum number of edges possible. These concepts are critical for practical applications in navigation systems, network routing, logistics optimization, and infrastructure design, where minimizing travel time, cost, or resource usage is of paramount importance.

Finding the shortest path within a network is crucial because it enables efficient travel and communication. In transportation networks, for example, determining the quickest route from one location to another can save time and resources. Similarly, in computer networks, the shortest path algorithm ensures that data packets travel along the most efficient route to minimize latency. Algorithms designed to compute shortest paths are also utilized in robotics for navigation and in mapping applications to compute optimal routes. These algorithms provide the foundation for many modern applications that handle real-time decision-making and resource distribution.

Dijkstra's algorithm is one of the most widely used methods for finding the shortest path in graphs with non-negative edge weights. The algorithm operates by iteratively selecting the vertex with the smallest known distance from the source and then relaxing the edges from this vertex, updating the distances of its neighboring vertices if a shorter path is found. The process begins by assigning an initial distance of zero to the source vertex and infinity to all other vertices. A priority queue is typically employed to efficiently retrieve the vertex with the minimum distance during each iteration. As edges are relaxed, the algorithm progressively builds a map of the shortest distances from the source to all reachable vertices. Once all vertices have been processed, the outcome is a complete shortest path tree rooted at the source.

The steps of Dijkstra's algorithm can be summarized as follows. First, initialize the distance for the source vertex to zero and set the distances for all other vertices to infinity. Next, insert the source vertex into a priority queue. Then, while the queue is not empty, extract the vertex with the smallest distance, and for each of its adjacent vertices, update the distance if a shorter path is found via this vertex. The key operation of the algorithm is edge relaxation, where the algorithm checks and potentially updates the cost associated with reaching each neighbor. This process continues until the priority queue is empty, ensuring that the shortest paths to all vertices have been discovered.

A practical demonstration of Dijkstra's algorithm is provided in the following Python code snippet. The implementation uses a simple graph representation via dictionaries and employs the heapq module for efficient priority queue operations:

```python
import heapq

def dijkstra(graph, source):
    # Initialize distances and priority queue
    distances = {vertex: float('infinity') for vertex in graph}
    distances[source] = 0
    priority_queue = [(0, source)]

    while priority_queue:
        current_distance, current_vertex = heapq.heappop(priority_queue)

        # If the distance is not the current shortest, skip it
        if current_distance > distances[current_vertex]:
            continue

        # Explore adjacent vertices
        for neighbor, weight in graph[current_vertex].items():
            distance = current_distance + weight
            # If a shorter path is found, update the neighbor's distance
            if distance < distances[neighbor]:
                distances[neighbor] = distance
                heapq.heappush(priority_queue, (distance, neighbor))

    return distances

# Example graph represented as an adjacency list with weights
graph = {
    'A': {'B': 5, 'C': 1},
    'B': {'A': 5, 'C': 2, 'D': 1},
    'C': {'A': 1, 'B': 2, 'D': 4, 'E': 8},
```

```
    'D': {'B': 1, 'C': 4, 'E': 3, 'F': 6},
    'E': {'C': 8, 'D': 3},
    'F': {'D': 6}
}
print(dijkstra(graph, 'A'))
```

The code demonstrates how distances from the source vertex are updated and how the priority queue efficiently manages the vertices yet to be processed. The time complexity of Dijkstra's algorithm, when implemented with a binary heap, is $O((V + E) \log V)$, where V is the number of vertices and E is the number of edges. This complexity reflects the overhead of maintaining and updating the priority queue and underscores the efficiency improvements achieved by using such data structures.

In parallel with the shortest path problem, spanning trees offer another important concept in graph theory. A spanning tree of a graph is a subgraph that includes all the vertices of the original graph and a subset of the edges, such that the subgraph is connected and acyclic. In many cases, the challenge lies in determining the minimum spanning tree (MST), which minimizes the total edge weight while still connecting all vertices. The MST is particularly important in designing network infrastructure, such as telecommunications, electrical grids, and transportation networks, where resources such as cable length, road distance, or overall cost need to be minimized.

Kruskal's algorithm is a popular method for constructing a minimum spanning tree. The algorithm operates by sorting all of the edges of the graph in non-decreasing order based on their weights. It then iteratively adds the smallest edge to the spanning tree, provided that the addition of the edge does not create a cycle. To efficiently detect cycles, a union-find data structure is typically used. This structure maintains a collection of disjoint sets, each representing a connected component, and the algorithm merges these sets as edges are added. The process continues until all vertices are included in a single connected component, resulting in the minimum spanning tree.

The implementation of Kruskal's algorithm can be broken down into distinct steps. Initially, sort all the edges by weight. Next, initialize a union-find data structure to manage disjoint sets for each vertex. Then, iterate through the sorted list of edges and for each edge, check whether the vertices it connects belong to different sets. If they do, include the edge in the MST and perform a union operation to merge the two sets. This continues until the spanning tree contains exactly $V - 1$ edges, where V is the total number of vertices in the graph.

An illustrative example of Kruskal's algorithm in Python is shown below. The code uses helper functions to implement union-find operations and demonstrates the process of building the minimum spanning tree:

```python
def find(parent, i):
    if parent[i] != i:
        parent[i] = find(parent, parent[i])
    return parent[i]

def union(parent, rank, x, y):
    root_x = find(parent, x)
    root_y = find(parent, y)
    if rank[root_x] < rank[root_y]:
        parent[root_x] = root_y
    elif rank[root_x] > rank[root_y]:
        parent[root_y] = root_x
    else:
        parent[root_y] = root_x
        rank[root_x] += 1

def kruskal(graph_edges, num_vertices):
    # Sort all edges in non-decreasing order of their weight
    graph_edges.sort(key=lambda item: item[2])
```

```
    parent = [i for i in range(num_vertices)]
    rank = [0] * num_vertices
    mst = []

    for edge in graph_edges:
        u, v, weight = edge
        root_u = find(parent, u)
        root_v = find(parent, v)

        # Check if adding this edge creates a cycle
        if root_u != root_v:
            mst.append(edge)
            union(parent, rank, root_u, root_v)

        # If MST contains (num_vertices - 1) edges, stop the process
        if len(mst) == num_vertices - 1:
            break

    return mst

# Example graph edges: (vertex1, vertex2, weight)
graph_edges = [
    (0, 1, 5), (0, 2, 1), (1, 2, 2),
    (1, 3, 1), (2, 3, 4), (2, 4, 8),
    (3, 4, 3), (3, 5, 6)
]
num_vertices = 6
mst = kruskal(graph_edges, num_vertices)
print(mst)
```

This code demonstrates the use of the union-find algorithm for cycle detection and the process of building the MST edge by edge. The overall time complexity of Kruskal's algorithm is $O(E \log E)$, which is dominated by the initial sorting of the edges. The additional union and find operations are performed in nearly constant time due to efficient union-find implementations with path compression and union by rank.

While Dijkstra's algorithm and Kruskal's algorithm operate in different realms of graph theory – one addressing the shortest path problem and the other constructing a spanning tree – both algorithms share common goals of optimizing performance and efficiency in network analysis. Dijkstra's algorithm is designed to find the shortest distance between nodes, focusing on the cost incurred along individual paths. In contrast, Kruskal's algorithm seeks to minimize the overall cost of connecting all nodes in a graph, ensuring that redundant or cyclical paths are eliminated. The methods employed by both algorithms have revolutionized how complex networks are managed and optimized, with practical applications spanning transportation, telecommunications, and computer science.

Comparing the two algorithms highlights the diversity of approaches in handling graph-based problems. Dijkstra's algorithm leverages a dynamic, iterative process based on edge relaxation and priority queues, while Kruskal's algorithm emphasizes sorting and the union-find structure to maintain optimal connectivity without cycles. Although both algorithms typically exhibit a time complexity proportional to $O(V + E)$ under ideal conditions, the specific implementation details and data structures used can significantly affect their performance in practical scenarios. Understanding these differences enables practitioners to select the most appropriate algorithm for the problem at hand, whether the objective is to find optimal paths or to efficiently construct a network backbone.

The integration of shortest path and spanning tree algorithms into real-world applications has had a transformative impact on technology and infrastructure. Navigation systems rely on shortest path algorithms to provide users with the fastest or most economical route between destinations, while network design and resource allocation increasingly depend on spanning tree concepts to minimize wiring and infrastructure costs. In both cases, the foundational principles of graph theory are directly applied to solve complex optimization problems, illustrating the pervasive influence of these techniques across diverse industries.

The exploration of Dijkstra's and Kruskal's algorithms thus serves not only to explain the mechanics of graph traversal and optimization but also to highlight the interplay between algorithm design and practical problem-solving. By ensuring efficient connectivity through minimal spanning trees and optimal pathfinding through shortest path algorithms, these methods underpin a wide range of modern technological advances. The challenges associated with these problems have driven innovation in data structures and algorithmic strategies, reinforcing the critical role of theoretical computer science in addressing real-world issues.

Through the analysis of these algorithms, it becomes evident that both the shortest path and the spanning tree problems are fundamental to efficient network design and optimization. The insights garnered from studying these approaches continue to influence contemporary research and application domains, ensuring that graph theory remains a vibrant and essential area of inquiry in the development of advanced computational systems.

6.4 Advanced Graph Algorithms

Advanced graph algorithms extend the basic principles of graph theory to address complex problems that arise in fields such as transportation, communication networks, and large-scale optimization. These advanced methods are designed not only to manage simple connectivity or traversal but also to solve intricate issues including network flows, connectivity, and resource optimization. In many real-world

189

applications, such advanced techniques form the backbone of systems that require robust, efficient, and scalable solutions to problems that involve the movement of resources or the detection of intricate structures within networks.

In practical terms, advanced graph algorithms are essential because they allow engineers and scientists to model and analyze systems where simple approaches do not suffice. For instance, modern transportation systems must manage dynamic traffic flows, ensuring that the movement of vehicles happens efficiently even under variable demand. Similarly, telecommunication networks require the efficient routing and transmission of data packets, often relying on sophisticated algorithms to manage network congestion and ensure reliable data delivery. These applications demand algorithms that not only determine connectivity and paths but also optimize flow and detect critical structural properties in complex networks.

One of the fundamental areas in advanced graph algorithms is the study of network flows. Network flows provide a model for representing the transportation or distribution of resources across a network composed of nodes and edges. In this model, nodes can represent locations or intersections, and weighted edges indicate the capacity or the maximum allowable flow between these nodes. The objective often revolves around maximizing the flow from a designated source node to a designated sink node, where each edge has an associated capacity that limits the amount of resource that can be transferred. This abstraction is vital in applications ranging from the design of water distribution systems to optimizing traffic in urban transportation networks.

Central to the study of network flows is the maximum flow problem. This problem entails determining the greatest possible flow that can be pushed from a source node to a sink node without violating the capacity constraints imposed on the edges. The maximum flow problem is not only about finding a viable distribution of flow but also about ensuring that the allocation is optimal, meaning that no additional resource can be transferred through the network without exceeding one or more of the capacity constraints. Solving this problem effectively is crucial when the goal is to utilize the available network capacity to its fullest potential.

A classical approach to solving the maximum flow problem is the Ford-Fulkerson method. This algorithm solves the problem by repeatedly searching for augmenting paths between the source and sink nodes and adjusting the flow along these paths until no further augmentations are possible. The essence of the Ford-Fulkerson method lies in its iterative process: it first identifies a path along which additional flow can be sent, then increases the overall flow by the smallest capacity found along that path, and finally updates the residual capacities of the network. The method continues this process until it reaches a state where there are no more augmenting paths available, and at that point, the maximum flow is achieved.

The Ford-Fulkerson algorithm operates through a series of well-defined steps. Initially, the network is set up with all capacities as given. An augmenting path is then sought, typically using a depth-first or breadth-first search strategy, from the source to the sink. Once a valid path is identified, the algorithm computes the bottleneck capacity—the minimum residual capacity along the path—and augments the flow by this amount. The capacities along the path are then updated: the forward edges decrease by the amount of the augmented flow, while reverse edges are incremented, setting up the possibility of flow cancellation in subsequent iterations if needed. This process iterates until no more augmenting paths can be found, ensuring that the maximum flow is achieved in the network.

A simple example of the Ford-Fulkerson method implemented in Python is provided below. The code demonstrates how the algorithm identifies augmenting paths, updates the residual capacities, and computes the maximum flow in a network represented by an adjacency matrix:

```
def ford_fulkerson(C, source, sink):
    n = len(C)
    flow = 0
    while True:
        # Find an augmenting path using DFS
        parent = [-1] * n
        stack = [source]
        parent[source] = source
        while stack and parent[sink] == -1:
            u = stack.pop()
            for v in range(n):
                if C[u][v] > 0 and parent[v] == -1:
                    parent[v] = u
                    stack.append(v)
        if parent[sink] == -1:
            break
        # Find the minimum capacity along the path
        v = sink
        increment = float('inf')
        while v != source:
            u = parent[v]
            increment = min(increment, C[u][v])
            v = u
        # Update residual capacities
        v = sink
        while v != source:
            u = parent[v]
            C[u][v] -= increment
            C[v][u] += increment
            v = u
        flow += increment
    return flow

# Example usage:
# C is the capacity matrix for the network.
```

192

```
C = [
    [0, 16, 13, 0, 0, 0],
    [0, 0, 10, 12, 0, 0],
    [0, 4, 0, 0, 14, 0],
    [0, 0, 9, 0, 0, 20],
    [0, 0, 0, 7, 0, 4],
    [0, 0, 0, 0, 0, 0]
]
max_flow = ford_fulkerson(C, 0, 5)
print("The maximum possible flow is", max_flow)
```

The algorithm above illustrates how augmenting paths are found and how the network is iteratively updated until the maximum flow from the source (vertex 0) to the sink (vertex 5) is determined. The time complexity of the Ford-Fulkerson method is influenced by the manner in which augmenting paths are found and the magnitude of the maximum flow itself. In the worst-case scenario, particularly when dealing with irrational capacities or when the algorithm chooses paths that result in very small increments, the number of iterations may become large, affecting the overall efficiency. However, for networks with integer capacities and when careful strategies such as using the Edmonds-Karp implementation (which employs breadth-first search) are applied, the method achieves a polynomial time complexity.

Beyond network flows, another key focus in advanced graph algorithms is the analysis of connectivity within graphs. Connectivity is a fundamental characteristic that pertains to the degree to which vertices in a graph are linked by edges. In many scenarios, it is critical to determine whether a graph is fully connected, meaning that there is a path between every pair of vertices, or to identify distinct subgraphs that are isolated from each other. Basic algorithms like DFS and BFS can be used to explore connectivity, but specialized algorithms are required when the task involves understanding the deeper structure of directed graphs or when the identification of strongly connected components is necessary.

Tarjan's algorithm represents one of the most efficient techniques for identifying strongly connected components (SCCs) within a directed graph. A strongly connected component is a subgraph in which every vertex is reachable from every other vertex within the same component. Tarjan's algorithm leverages depth-first search (DFS) in conjunction with additional bookkeeping to record the order in which vertices are visited and to track low-link values, which indicate the earliest visited vertex reachable from a given vertex. Through this process, the algorithm efficiently partitions the graph into its strongly connected components in a single pass.

The steps of Tarjan's algorithm involve initiating a DFS from each unvisited vertex, recording the discovery time and low-link value for each vertex, and using a stack to keep track of the recursion. When the algorithm backtracks, if a vertex is found to be the root of a strongly connected component—meaning its discovery time equals its low-link value—the vertices are then popped off the stack until the root is reached, marking a complete component. This approach ensures that all SCCs are identified in an efficient manner, and the algorithm achieves a linear time complexity of $O(V + E)$, where V is the number of vertices and E is the number of edges.

The discussion of advanced graph algorithms thus extends to both the domain of network flows and connectivity. The methodical process of augmenting flows using the Ford-Fulkerson method and the identification of connected components through Tarjan's algorithm illustrate the breadth of challenges that advanced algorithms tackle. The Ford-Fulkerson method addresses the practical need to maximize throughput in networks, while Tarjan's algorithm ensures that complex directed graphs can be decomposed into manageable and analyzable components.

These techniques are not only theoretical exercises but have practical implications in numerous real-world applications. In transportation networks, for example, advanced flow algorithms can optimize the distribution of resources such as fuel and goods, ensuring that bottlenecks are resolved and that the transportation system operates at maximum efficiency. Similarly, in computer networks, advanced algorithms ensure that data packets travel through paths that maximize throughput and minimize congestion, leading to improved overall performance. In addition, the ability to swiftly identify strongly connected components in directed graphs has significant applications in social network analysis and web page ranking, where the relationships between entities are complex and dynamic.

The integration of these advanced methods into practical systems underlines their importance in supporting modern infrastructure and communication systems. As networks continue to grow in complexity and scale, the need for advanced graph algorithms becomes ever more pronounced. The methods discussed here—from maximizing network flow with Ford-Fulkerson to efficiently decomposing graphs with Tarjan's algorithm—provide the foundation for developing systems that are robust, efficient, and capable of handling the demands of contemporary applications.

Advanced graph algorithms serve as indispensable tools in the analysis and optimization of complex networks. Their ability to model, examine, and solve problems related to network flows and connectivity is critical in a wide array of fields, ensuring that systems are both efficient and resilient. The study of these algorithms not only deepens one's understanding of graph theory but also equips practitioners with the methodologies needed to address some of the most challenging problems in modern technology.

6.5 Applications of Graphs

Graph theory serves as a robust framework for modeling and solving a diverse array of real-world problems. At its core, the application of graph theory involves representing complex systems as networks comprised of nodes and edges, which correspond to entities and the relationships between them. This abstraction enables researchers and practitioners to interpret, analyze, and optimize systems in fields ranging from transportation to biology. The versatility of graphs makes them ideal for addressing problems where connectivity and relationships are central to the problem domain.

One prominent application of graph theory is in the modeling and optimization of transportation networks. Transportation systems, whether they involve roadways, flight paths, or public transit routes, rely heavily on efficient routing and connectivity to minimize travel time and costs. In such networks, vertices represent locations such as cities, intersections, or transit stops, while edges symbolize the roads, air routes, or rail lines that interconnect these points. Analysis of these networks using graph algorithms can yield optimal routing strategies, shortest path calculations, and insights into potential bottlenecks or vulnerabilities. By simulating traffic flow and transit schedules, graph-based models help urban planners design more resilient and efficient transportation infrastructures.

The same principles extend naturally to the study of social networks. In social network analysis, individuals are typically modeled as nodes, and their interactions or relationships are represented as edges. Graph algorithms enable the mapping of friendships, collaborations, or influence patterns among users. This analysis can reveal clusters of tightly-knit communities, central figures within networks, and the overall structure of social interactions. By quantifying attributes such as centrality and connectivity, graph-based methods provide valuable insights for applications ranging from marketing strategies to the spread of information or misinformation within communities.

Beyond social networks, graph-based models are integral to the functioning of search engines. The web is, in essence, a vast graph where webpages act as nodes and hyperlinks function as edges connecting these nodes. Search engines leverage this interconnected structure to evaluate the authority and relevance of pages through algorithms that consider the quantity and quality of links pointing to and from each webpage. By analyzing these interconnections, graph-based search algorithms improve the ranking of search results, helping users find the most pertinent information quickly and efficiently.

The importance of graphs is not confined to the digital realm; they also play a critical role in modeling the topology of the internet and communication networks. The network topology of the internet—a massive web of interconnected servers, routers, and communication links—is effectively captured using graphs. In these models, nodes represent network devices or servers, and edges denote the physical or virtual connections between them. Understanding this structure is fundamental for network engineers who aim to ensure robustness, optimize data routing, and maintain fault tolerance. Graph algorithms help identify critical nodes whose failure may cause widespread disruptions, thereby guiding improvements in network security and maintenance procedures.

Another area where graph theory is extensively applied is in the development of recommendation systems. Online retailers, streaming services, and social media platforms utilize graph algorithms to analyze relationships between users and products or content. In these systems, the nodes might represent users, items, or even specific features of items, while edges capture interactions, similarities, or preferences. By examining the structure of this graph, recommendation engines can suggest products or content that align with a user's interests based on their behavior and the behavior of similar users. This graph-based approach lends itself to more personalized and accurate recommendations, ultimately enhancing user engagement and satisfaction.

Graph theory also finds applications in the realm of biological networks. In molecular biology and bioinformatics, proteins, genes, and metabolic pathways are often modeled as graphs. Nodes represent biological entities such as proteins or genes, and edges represent the interactions or regulatory relationships between them. Analyzing these networks enables scientists to uncover critical interactions that drive cellular processes, identify potential targets for drug development, and understand the complexities of metabolic and genetic pathways. The power of graph algorithms in this context lies in their ability to manage the high levels of interconnectedness inherent in biological systems, giving researchers the tools needed to navigate the complexities of life at the molecular level.

Routing algorithms, which are essential for efficient data transmission and navigation in networks, are closely intertwined with graph theory. Techniques such as Dijkstra's algorithm and the A* search algorithm are classic examples of how graph traversal can be harnessed to compute the most efficient paths in a network. In telecommunications, these algorithms help determine optimal routes for data packets across the internet, thereby minimizing latency and maximizing throughput. Similarly, in navigation systems, route planning algorithms use graphs to calculate not only the shortest distance between two points but also consider real-time factors such as traffic congestion and road conditions. The continuous evolution of these routing techniques reflects the ever-growing demands of modern communication and navigation systems.

Graph models also serve a significant role in the field of game theory. In competitive scenarios such as strategic board games or economic models, graphs can represent the myriad interactions and possible outcomes based on different strategies. In this framework, nodes may correspond to possible states or decisions, and edges represent transitions resulting from specific moves or actions. By analyzing these graphs, theorists can evaluate strategies, determine equilibrium conditions, and predict competitive behavior. The insights gained from applying graph theory to game theory have broad implications, impacting fields as varied as economics, political science, and evolutionary biology.

The influence of graph algorithms is further evident in machine learning, where they contribute substantially to tasks involving clustering, classification, and even dimensionality reduction. In clustering methods, graphs are constructed where nodes represent data points and edges denote similarity metrics between points. Algorithms such as spectral clustering analyze the structure of these graphs to partition data into meaningful clusters. Additionally, graph-based semi-supervised learning techniques leverage the relationships encoded in graphs to improve classification accuracy, particularly in situations where labeled data is scarce. This capability to capture and exploit the underlying structure of data makes graph algorithms a powerful tool in modern machine learning applications, opening new avenues for research and practical deployment.

The multidisciplinary reach of graph theory can be seen in its application to legal studies, epidemiology, and risk management as well. For instance, in legal studies and social sciences, graphs are used to map interrelationships between individuals or entities, providing clarity on networks of influence or collusion. In epidemiology, models of disease transmission leverage graph theory to simulate how infectious diseases spread through populations. By examining the connectivity and interaction patterns within a community, public health officials can predict outbreak dynamics and devise control strategies. Similarly, risk management models in finance rely on graphs to understand and mitigate systemic risk within interconnected markets and institutions.

Graph applications extend into the realm of environmental science as well, where they help model and optimize resource distribution in ecosystems. Graph models can represent the flow of nutrients, water, or energy through an ecosystem, allowing scientists to analyze the stability and resilience of these systems under various stress scenarios. Understanding these flows is critical for developing strategies to conserve biodiversity and manage natural resources sustainably.

In synthesizing the numerous applications of graph theory across disciplines, it becomes clear that the practical value of graphs lies in their simplicity and power. The elegant abstraction of nodes and edges provides a universal language for describing and solving problems that involve complex associations and interdependencies. Whether it is optimizing a transportation network, dissecting the structure of a social network, or unraveling the intricacies of biological interactions, graph theory offers a powerful and flexible toolkit for turning abstract relationships into actionable insights.

The diverse applications of graphs underscore the interdisciplinary nature of modern problem-solving. The ability to model real-world systems as graphs not only simplifies the computational challenges involved but also enables the integration of disparate datasets and domain expertise into unified analytical frameworks. This synergy has profound implications: by leveraging graph algorithms, researchers and practitioners can uncover hidden patterns, predict system behavior, and make informed decisions that have a tangible impact on society.

The exploration of graph applications demonstrates that these techniques are far more than theoretical constructs; they are indispensable in solving real-world problems. Their widespread adoption in areas such as transportation, social networking, internet topology, recommendation systems, biology, routing, game theory, and machine learning testifies to their efficacy and adaptability. As our world becomes increasingly interconnected, the role of graph theory is only set to expand, driving innovations across technology, science, and engineering.

7

Algorithm Analysis and Optimization

This chapter delves into the critical aspects of evaluating and improving algorithm performance through analysis and optimization techniques. It begins by examining complexity notations, such as Big O, Big Theta, and Big Omega, which help quantify algorithm efficiency in terms of time and space. The discussion includes various optimization techniques designed to refine algorithms for enhanced performance, focusing on solving practical issues related to runtime and resource usage. Additionally, the chapter introduces profiling and empirical methods as tools for validating performance analyses in real-world scenarios. Ultimately, it stresses the importance of continuous optimization in developing effective and efficient software solutions.

7.1   Complexity Notations and Analysis

Complexity notation is a mathematical framework used to evaluate the performance of an algorithm in terms of resources—primarily time and memory space—as a function of the input size. This framework provides an essential means to measure how algorithm efficiency scales and is central to both the analysis and design of software. In this section, we present a detailed discussion of complexity notations, beginning with the foundational concept and continuing with an exploration of specific notations and their practical implications for algorithm performance.

Understanding complexity notation begins with its definition as a formal language that quantifies the behavior of algorithms. At its core, complexity notation abstracts the precise number of operations or the memory usage into mathematical terms, discarding constants and lower-order terms so that the dominant aspect of an algorithm's performance is highlighted. This abstraction is vital because it allows algorithms with different running times to be compared by concentrating solely on their growth rates when faced with very large inputs.

The importance of analyzing algorithm complexity cannot be overstated. Measuring complexity enables developers and researchers to make informed design decisions, ensuring that the chosen approach remains scalable and efficient as problem sizes expand. By understanding the performance characteristics, one can pinpoint the parts of an algorithm that consume excessive computational resources, thereby guiding efforts in optimization. This analysis supports a rational basis for selecting one algorithm over another when multiple solutions are available, balancing trade-offs between speed and memory consump-

tion. In practical software design, complexity analysis also helps anticipate potential bottlenecks and implement corrective strategies before
deploying an application at scale.

A primary component of complexity notation is Big O notation, which
describes the upper bound of an algorithm's runtime. Big O notation is
used to characterize the worst-case scenario, communicating an upper
limit on the number of steps an algorithm takes as the size of the input
grows. Essentially, Big O provides a guarantee; regardless of the input,
the algorithm will not exceed a specific growth rate. When we refer
to an algorithm as $O(n)$ or $O(n^2)$, we are specifying that its runtime
increases linearly or quadratically with the input size in the worst-case
scenario, respectively. This perspective is invaluable when one must
ensure robust performance even under maximum load conditions.

The abstraction provided by Big O notation is achieved by discarding
lower-order terms and constant factors. For example, if an algorithm
has a runtime expressed as $5n^2 + 3n + 10$, the dominant factor as n becomes large is n^2. In Big O terms, this algorithm is classified as $O(n^2)$
because the quadratic term overshadows the linear and constant components. By focusing on the most significant contributor to the overall
complexity, Big O notation simplifies the evaluation of an algorithm's
efficiency, facilitating easier comparison among competing solutions.
This focus on asymptotic behavior is especially important when theoretical performance must be gauged in scenarios with immense input
sizes.

Several common examples illustrate the practical implications of Big
O notation. For instance, constant time complexity, denoted by $O(1)$,
implies that the execution time of the algorithm is independent of the
input size. This typically occurs in cases where a single operation,
such as accessing a specific data element in an array, is performed.

In contrast, an algorithm that requires scanning through all elements in a list exhibits linear time complexity, $O(n)$, indicating that its runtime scales directly with the number of items. More complex operations, such as sorting via simple comparison techniques, may express quadratic behavior, $O(n^2)$, reflecting an increase in operations proportional to the square of the input size. Additionally, logarithmic complexity, $O(\log n)$, is characteristic of algorithms that repeatedly reduce the problem size by a constant factor, such as binary search. These examples not only define the complexity classes but also highlight the significant performance differences that can arise between them.

Beyond Big O, Big Theta notation offers a more precise characterization of algorithm performance by providing a tight bound—both upper and lower—on the runtime. Big Theta notation describes the exact asymptotic behavior of an algorithm. When an algorithm is classified as $\Theta(n)$, it implies that its runtime grows linearly with the input size and that this growth rate represents both the upper and lower bounds. This precise match between observed performance and theoretical evaluation is crucial when modeling algorithms that exhibit consistent behavior across different input scenarios.

Complementing Big Theta notation is Big Omega notation, which sets a lower bound on algorithm performance. This notation describes the best-case scenario, indicating the minimum amount of work that an algorithm must perform regardless of optimizations or particularly favorable conditions. For example, if an algorithm has a best-case runtime of $\Omega(n)$, it tells us that there is no possibility of the algorithm performing faster than linear time, even under the most ideal conditions. Understanding Big Omega is particularly useful when analyzing algorithms with performance characteristics that vary depending on the nature of the input.

When examining complexity notations, it is useful to consider various complexity classes such as constant, linear, quadratic, logarithmic, and exponential. Each of these classes reveals distinct insights into algorithm efficiency. Constant complexity $O(1)$ suggests minimal dependence on the input, whereas linear $O(n)$ and quadratic $O(n^2)$ describe progressively larger increases in resource demands. Logarithmic complexity $O(\log n)$ offers an appealing balance by ensuring that even significant increases in input size yield only incremental increases in computation time, while exponential complexity $O(2^n)$ is indicative of algorithms that become impractical quickly as input sizes grow. Awareness of these classes informs the selection and design of algorithms, particularly when identifying practical limits and optimization opportunities.

The techniques used to assess an algorithm's time complexity typically involve counting the number of operations performed and, in certain cases, solving recurrence relations to predict performance, especially in recursive algorithms. Operation counting is straightforward in iterative algorithms, where one can deduce how many times a specific block of code executes relative to the input size. In recursive algorithms, recurrence relations model the reductions in problem size and the number of recursive calls, which can then be solved to reveal the growth rate. Both analytical methods require a detailed understanding of the algorithm's structure and a methodical approach to breaking down its operations into countable units.

In parallel with time complexity, space complexity is another critical metric that measures the amount of memory used by an algorithm. This analysis includes not only the space required to store the input data but also any auxiliary storage that the algorithm may need during execution. Evaluating space complexity typically involves identifying the primary data structures used and quantifying their memory footprint as a function of the input size. Such examination is essential in environments with limited memory or when optimizing for both speed and memory consumption is a priority.

Visualizing these complexity notations can significantly aid in understanding their differences and relationships. The table below provides a comparative overview of various complexity classes, illustrating how their growth rates differ as input sizes increase.

Complexity Class	Growth Behavior	Typical Example
$O(1)$	Constant	Array indexing
$O(\log n)$	Logarithmic	Binary search
$O(n)$	Linear	Single loop over an array
$O(n^2)$	Quadratic	Nested loops (simple sorting)
$O(2^n)$	Exponential	Recursive solution to the Tower of Hanoi

Table 7.1: *Comparison of common complexity classes and their growth behaviors as the input size increases.*

Techniques for analyzing both time and space complexity are fundamental to understanding an algorithm's overall performance. Detailed time complexity analysis may involve direct mathematical computation or empirical measurements such as profiling, where an algorithm's runtime is observed over various input sizes to determine its scaling behavior. For operation counting, every major loop and recursive call is examined to determine its contribution to the total execution time. Similarly, for space complexity analysis, every memory allocation, be it fixed storage for static variables or dynamic storage allocations, is carefully accounted for.

The discussion of time and space complexity coalesces into a central insight: evaluating an algorithm's performance requires considering both runtime and memory management. An algorithm that executes

208

rapidly may still be inefficient if it utilizes excessive memory, and conversely, an algorithm optimized for memory usage may be too slow for practical use. Striking a balance between these factors is crucial when optimizing resource usage, especially in environments with strict constraints or where real-time responses are required.

Throughout this discussion, the nuances of Big O, Big Theta, and Big Omega notations provide a robust framework for algorithm analysis. Big O notation conveys the worst-case resource consumption, Big Theta offers an exact representation of an algorithm's asymptotic behavior, and Big Omega sets the lower bound for performance expectations. Moreover, classifying algorithms into distinct complexity classes clarifies performance evaluations and guides decisions on optimization strategies and algorithm selection.

By analyzing time complexity through operation counting and solving recurrence relations, and by rigorously tracking space complexity, one can systematically identify inefficiencies that may compromise system performance. The combined use of theoretical models and empirical measurements forms a cornerstone for evaluating algorithms in both computational theory and software engineering.

The examination of complexity notations is central to the development of effective and efficient algorithms. These insights demystify the behavior of algorithms under different conditions and provide concrete data to guide optimization. Grounding performance discussions in robust mathematical principles, complemented by clear comparative visualizations, equips professionals with the tools to critically assess and refine algorithmic solutions.

7.2 Time and Space Complexity

Time and space complexity are crucial metrics for evaluating algorithm efficiency by assessing how the runtime and memory consumption of an algorithm scale with the size of its input. In this context, time complexity is a measure that is used to quantify the number of operations an algorithm performs, while space complexity quantifies the memory required during its execution. Both metrics are indispensable in ensuring that a given algorithm is well-suited for the demands of practical applications and can perform optimally even as the volumes of data increase.

The analysis of runtime performance is of primary importance because it directly affects application responsiveness and user experience. An algorithm that executes quickly on small inputs may become prohibitively slow as the input size grows, leading to unresponsive software or even system failures in extreme cases. As a result, analyzing time complexity allows developers to predict the behavior of an algorithm under different loads. This prediction is essential when selecting an appropriate algorithm for tasks that range from real-time processing in user interfaces to high-volume batch processing in distributed systems.

Time complexity describes the growth rate of the runtime relative to the size of the input data. It provides a high-level understanding of an algorithm's performance by abstracting away constant factors and lower order terms. By expressing runtime in terms of input size, one can compare algorithms independently of hardware specifics. Even though an algorithm with a low constant factor might seem efficient for small inputs, asymptotic analysis reveals that an algorithm with a poor growth rate might become inefficient or even unusable as input sizes increase significantly.

Various methods exist for measuring the time complexity of an algorithm. One common approach is analytical computation, where a mathematical model of the algorithm is constructed by counting the significant operations performed during its execution. This method often involves creating a recurrence relation for recursive algorithms or simply summing loop executions in iterative algorithms. Asymptotic analysis then allows the derivation of a simplified expression, commonly stated using Big O notation, that captures the upper bound of the algorithm's growth rate.

Another effective method is empirical timing, where the actual execution time of an algorithm is measured using performance counters or timers. This practical approach is particularly useful when theoretical analysis is cumbersome or when the algorithm involves various system-level interactions that impact performance. By measuring the wall-clock time for different input sizes, it is possible to generate a performance curve, thereby validating or complementing the theoretical model. Both approaches, analytical and empirical, are critical in understanding an algorithm's true performance characteristics.

For instance, consider a simple code snippet that demonstrates how one might use a timer in a programming environment to analyze the runtime of an algorithm. The following example uses a timing function to measure the duration of a loop that simulates a computationally intensive task:

```
import time

def simulated_algorithm(n):
    total = 0
    for i in range(n):
```

211

```
        total += i   # Simple operation simulating workload
    return total

# Measure the execution time for different input sizes
input_sizes = [1000, 10000, 100000]
for n in input_sizes:
    start_time = time.perf_counter()
    result = simulated_algorithm(n)
    end_time = time.perf_counter()
    print(f"Input Size: {n}, Result: {result}, Time: {end_time -
    start_time:.6f} seconds")
```

In the above code, the function `simulated_algorithm` represents an algorithm whose runtime is expected to change linearly with the input size. The snippet uses a high-resolution performance counter to measure the time taken for each loop execution, thereby providing empirical evidence of time complexity. This technique is useful not only for verifying theoretical predictions but also for benchmarking code optimizations and calibrating system performance.

Beyond runtime, the evaluation of an algorithm's memory usage, or space complexity, is equally critical. Space complexity encompasses both the memory required to store the input and any additional memory allocated during execution (auxiliary space). Efficient memory usage is particularly significant in constrained environments, such as embedded systems or mobile devices, where available resources are limited. Moreover, excessive memory consumption can lead to increased overhead from system resource management, such as paging and cache misses, which may further impact runtime performance.

Understanding space complexity involves quantifying all memory allocations that occur during the execution of an algorithm. This includes fixed memory allocations, such as variables that maintain constant size regardless of input, as well as variable allocations that scale with input size. For instance, an algorithm that creates a new array based on the input size will exhibit variable space complexity, while simple arithmetic operations typically require constant space. Analyzing these aspects is vital for ensuring that a program remains efficient and does not exhaust available memory during its operation.

Several common types of space complexity can be identified. Fixed space complexity refers to algorithms whose memory usage remains constant, independent of input size. In contrast, variable space complexity describes situations where memory consumption increases in tandem with input size. Efficient algorithm design involves carefully selecting data structures and managing memory allocation so that the additional space required is minimized, thereby improving overall performance.

To analyze space complexity, developers often track memory allocations during execution, either by direct inspection of code behavior or by using profiling tools. Profiling tools can capture peak memory usage and help identify memory-intensive portions of the algorithm. This analysis is especially important when processing large data sets, where poor memory management could lead to system crashes or significantly slower performance due to increased garbage collection or memory swapping.

Consider the following example that illustrates a simple algorithm designed to analyze its own space usage. This sample code creates a new list whose size scales with the input and demonstrates how additional memory requirements can be tracked:

```
def generate_list(n):
    # Create a list of n elements
    data = [i for i in range(n)]
    return data
```

```
# Analyze space usage by generating lists of different sizes
input_sizes = [1000, 10000, 100000]
for n in input_sizes:
    generated_data = generate_list(n)
    print(f"Generated list with {len(generated_data)} elements")
```

In this example, memory usage grows linearly with the input size, as evident from the dynamic allocation of list elements. Although this code snippet does not measure memory consumption directly, it serves to illustrate the principle that increasing input sizes will proportionally increase the memory footprint of the algorithm. Practical measurement of space complexity may involve using specialized profilers or operating system tools that capture accurate memory usage statistics.

Balancing time and space complexity is a central challenge in algorithm design. Often, there is a trade-off between the two: optimizing an algorithm for faster runtime might require additional memory, whereas memory-efficient algorithms might perform slower. The goal is, therefore, to achieve a balanced approach where both runtime and memory usage are optimized for the specific requirements of the application. For example, in systems where memory is a scarce resource, it might be preferable to choose an algorithm that uses less memory even if its runtime is slightly longer, and vice versa.

The practical significance of measuring both forms of complexity extends beyond academic interest. In real-world applications, input sizes can be vast, and the hardware on which these algorithms run might have limited processing power and memory. Thus, understanding and optimizing these metrics is essential for building robust applications. Moreover, hardware trends such as multicore processors and increased memory capacities have led to new paradigms in algorithm design where both parallel execution and efficient memory management are key considerations.

An effective strategy for mitigating performance issues is to use a combination of analytical methods and empirical testing. Analytical models provide a theoretical baseline, but empirical timing helps validate these models under real-world conditions. Similarly, while a mathematical analysis of space requirements can predict memory usage patterns, profiling during execution provides concrete data that can inform further optimizations.

As developers apply these techniques, they must also consider the broader context of their application. The decision to optimize for time may be influenced by factors such as user interface responsiveness, while space optimization may be dictated by the operating environment. In distributed systems, for instance, network latency might play as crucial a role as computational complexity, and thus the overall performance must be assessed in context.

By integrating the concepts of time and space complexity into the development process, software engineers can make informed decisions that strike a balance between fast execution times and efficient memory usage. This integration leads to the creation of software that not only performs well under ideal conditions but also maintains its efficiency as workloads scale. Such balanced design is essential for building applications that are both high-performing and resource-efficient.

The exploration of time and space complexity in algorithm analysis provides a comprehensive framework for evaluating performance. It emphasizes the necessity of measuring both runtime and memory requirements and introduces the common methodologies used to perform these measurements. Whether by calculating the number of operations through analytical methods or by conducting empirical tests

215

with timers and performance counters, these techniques equip the developer with a clear understanding of the algorithm's behavior under varying conditions.

In practice, both strong theoretical foundations and empirical evidence converge to guide developers toward optimal algorithm choices. By adhering to well-established principles and employing practical measurement techniques, one can ensure that an algorithm is not only correct but also efficient and scalable. The insights gained from such analyses are indispensable for the continuous improvement of software systems, as they provide actionable data that can be used to refine code, enhance system performance, and ultimately deliver better user experiences.

7.3   Optimization Techniques

Optimization techniques encompass a variety of methods aimed at refining algorithms to achieve enhanced performance and efficiency. These methods target the reduction of execution time and resource consumption, ensuring that an algorithm functions effectively, even when scaled to handle larger or more complex data sets. At the outset, optimization is defined as the process of improving the efficiency of an algorithm by modifying its implementation, data handling, or underlying logic. The goal is to achieve a reduction in running time while simultaneously decreasing memory or other resource usage without compromising the algorithm's correctness or output integrity.

Algorithm optimization holds significant importance in the realm of software development, particularly in environments where computing resources are limited or when high-performance applications are required. In resource-constrained systems, such as embedded devices or mobile applications, optimization directly influences the feasibility and overall user experience. Even in scenarios where resources seem abundant, inefficient algorithms can lead to excessive energy consumption, slower execution times, and suboptimal performance under heavy loads. Hence, a carefully optimized algorithm not only contributes to scalability but also ensures that the software remains responsive and reliable as the volume of processed data increases.

A fundamental step toward algorithm optimization is the identification of bottlenecks—sections within the algorithm that disproportionately affect performance. Techniques such as profiling and performance analysis are crucial in this stage. Profiling involves instrumenting the code to monitor its behavior during execution, thereby exposing periods of high computational intensity or excessive memory usage. Profilers can detect which functions or loops require optimization and help isolate redundant operations or unnecessary computations. This data-driven approach provides a practical starting point for targeted improvements, allowing developers to focus on modifying the parts of the algorithm that yield the highest returns in performance gains.

Once bottlenecks are identified, code refactoring becomes an essential tool in the optimization process. Refactoring is the structural reorganization of the codebase without altering its external behavior or output. Through refactoring, developers can simplify complex logic, eliminate redundant code, and rewrite inefficient constructs into more streamlined versions. Such modifications often lead to a reduction in execution time, particularly when dealing with repeated processes or recursive calls. The process of refactoring not only improves performance but also enhances code readability and maintainability, making long-term development and future optimization efforts more manageable.

Selecting efficient data structures is another critical factor in optimizing algorithm performance. The choice of data structures has a significant impact on both time and space complexity. For example, using a hash table for search operations typically results in constant time complexity ($O(1)$) compared to linear time complexity ($O(n)$) when using an unsorted list. The proper alignment of data structures with the operations being performed can dramatically reduce overhead and improve overall efficiency. In cases where data retrieval speed is paramount, choosing data structures that minimize the need for repetitive scanning or unnecessary iterations is crucial. This careful selection often involves analyzing the nature of the problem and determining which structure—from arrays and linked lists to trees and graphs—best supports the required operations.

Beyond low-level code improvements and data structure selection, various algorithmic techniques can serve as alternative strategies for optimization. Greedy methods, for instance, focus on making the optimal local choice at each step and can offer significant performance improvements in problems where such approaches yield near-optimal global solutions. Dynamic programming is another powerful technique, especially when dealing with problems that exhibit overlapping subproblems. By storing intermediate results through tabulation or memoization, dynamic programming avoids redundant calculations and improves efficiency markedly. Additionally, divide-and-conquer strategies, when applicable, break problems into smaller, more manageable subproblems that are easier and faster to solve individually. These algorithmic paradigms provide a framework for rethinking the problem in ways that reduce complexity and computation time.

Caching and memoization are specific techniques that further enhance efficiency by storing previously computed values. When an algorithm encounters the same state repeatedly, caching prevents the need for duplicate calculations by retrieving precomputed results from memory. This approach is particularly effective in recursive algorithms or when processing overlapping subproblems where the same computations occur multiple times. By trading off a small amount of additional memory usage, caching offers a significant speedup, ensuring that the algorithm does not waste valuable computational resources on redundant operations.

Parallelization represents another cornerstone in modern algorithm optimization. The concept involves dividing tasks into subtasks that can be executed concurrently across multiple cores or processors. In today's computing environments, where multicore processors are the norm, parallel processing can drastically reduce overall execution times for algorithms that are amenable to such treatment. Parallelization requires careful consideration to avoid issues such as race conditions and deadlocks, but when implemented correctly, it facilitates the handling of larger data sets and more computationally intensive tasks in a fraction of the time required by sequential processing. The use of thread pools, distributed computing frameworks, and concurrent data structures all contribute to effective parallel algorithm design.

In some cases, finding an exact optimal solution to a problem may be computationally prohibitive. Approximation algorithms offer a practical alternative by providing near-optimal solutions with considerably reduced computation times. These algorithms employ heuristics or probabilistic methods to achieve results that are close to the best possible answer. While approximation techniques may sacrifice some degree of accuracy, they are particularly valuable in complex or NP-hard problems where exact solutions are impractical. By accepting a minor margin of error, approximation algorithms enable applications to deliver results within acceptable bounds while maintaining high performance.

Performance testing plays a pivotal role throughout the optimization process. Systematic testing and benchmarking assess the impact of each optimization strategy and verify that improvements translate into measurable enhancements under realistic conditions. Performance tests often simulate a variety of scenarios, including best-case, worst-case, and average-case inputs, to ensure that the optimized algorithm performs reliably across diverse conditions. Tools such as automated benchmark suites and performance profilers provide essential data that inform iterative refinements and confirm that each change results in tangible improvements. These tests not only validate the effectiveness of the optimization strategies but also help diagnose potential regressions introduced during the refactoring process.

Maintaining clear documentation throughout the optimization process is equally important. Detailed records of the changes made, the rationale behind each optimization, and the observed performance gains serve as a valuable resource for future development. Good documentation ensures that the optimization strategy is transparent and reproducible, facilitating maintenance and further enhancements. It also provides new developers a roadmap for understanding past decisions and learning from previous successes and challenges. Consistently updated documentation supports ongoing optimization efforts and aids in troubleshooting any issues that arise from subsequent modifications.

The variety of techniques discussed here—from profiling and bottleneck identification to code refactoring, efficient data structure selection, and advanced algorithmic strategies—underscores the continuous nature of performance refinement. Algorithm optimization is not a one-off task but an iterative process that evolves alongside the software and its usage environment. As new challenges and requirements emerge, previously optimized algorithms may require further adjustments, reinforcing the need for a flexible and systematic approach to performance improvement. Whether through simple code modifications or the implementation of sophisticated parallel processing strategies, the ultimate aim is to develop algorithms that are both effective and efficient in real-world applications.

By prioritizing the identification of bottlenecks and methodically applying optimization techniques, it is possible to significantly enhance the performance of algorithms. The emphasis on code refactoring and the strategic use of data structures ensures that software is both robust and scalable. Incorporating algorithmic techniques such as greedy methods and dynamic programming, together with caching, memoization, and parallelization, further refines computational processes and reduces overall resource consumption. Approximation algorithms add an additional layer of practicality by delivering near-optimal results when exact computations are infeasible due to high complexity.

Comprehensive performance testing and meticulous documentation serve as the backbone of any successful optimization effort. They ensure that the improvements are not only conceptual but also empirically validated and easy to maintain over time. In practical terms, these techniques enable developers to address performance issues proactively and iteratively, leading to software that is better equipped to handle increasing workloads and complex processing tasks.

Ultimately, the strategies for optimizing algorithms discussed in this section are interdependent and mutually reinforcing. Each technique contributes to reducing execution times and resource utilization, thereby creating a more responsive and efficient system overall. The continuous nature of performance refinement calls for an ongoing commitment to monitoring and improving algorithm performance, ensuring that software solutions remain both agile and robust in the face of evolving technology and user demands. Through this integrated approach to optimization, developers can build systems that not only meet the immediate requirements of current applications but also anticipate and adapt to future challenges without sacrificing efficiency or scalability.

7.4   Profiling and Empirical Methods

Profiling and empirical methods are practical techniques used to measure the performance of algorithms under real-world conditions. These methods provide a way to validate theoretical analysis by capturing how software behaves during execution. Unlike pure analytical models that focus solely on algorithmic complexity, profiling involves instrumenting the code to monitor its runtime characteristics, memory usage, and input/output operations to gain a detailed view of the actual performance. Empirical testing complements this approach by subjecting algorithms to standardized scenarios, which allows developers to benchmark their performance against defined metrics. Together, these techniques ensure that performance improvements are not merely conjectural but are supported by data gathered from realistic operating environments.

The importance of profiling cannot be overemphasized in the context of modern software development. By employing profiling methods, developers can identify performance bottlenecks, areas where the code consumes excessive computational resources, or regions where memory is used inefficiently. Profiling thus forms the basis for targeted optimization by turning abstract performance metrics into actionable insights. For instance, through CPU profiling, one might discover that a particular loop or function is responsible for a significant portion of the overall runtime. Similarly, memory profiling may reveal unanticipated leaks or spikes in usage that could degrade system performance. In essence, profiling converts high-level performance issues into concrete data that guide developers on where to concentrate their optimization efforts, ensuring the software remains both responsive and resource-efficient.

Benchmarking is a closely related concept that involves running standardized tests to evaluate algorithm performance against predetermined metrics. A benchmark is essentially a controlled experiment in which an algorithm's performance is measured under consistent conditions, such that results are both repeatable and comparable across different implementations. For effective benchmarking, certain criteria must be met: the tests should be repeatable, meaning that running them multiple times under the same conditions produces consistent results; they should be accurate, capturing precise measurements of runtime, memory, or other resource consumption; and they must be relevant, simulating real-world conditions to provide meaningful data about how an algorithm will perform in production scenarios. When these criteria are satisfied, benchmarking offers a reliable foundation for comparing different algorithms or for tracking performance improvements over time.

A range of profiling techniques is available to assess various aspects of algorithm performance. CPU profiling focuses on measuring the time spent executing different portions of the code, revealing which functions or lines are most computationally intensive. Memory profiling provides insights into how much memory is allocated, identifying both the quantity and duration of memory usage. I/O profiling, on the other hand, monitors operations related to disk and network access, which can often be a hidden factor in performance degradation. Each of these techniques employs specialized tools and methodologies tailored to the particular facet of performance they address. By combining results from these different profiling methods, developers obtain a multi-dimensional view of algorithm efficiency, allowing them to pinpoint specific areas that contribute disproportionately to overall resource consumption.

Profile-guided optimization (PGO) is an advanced strategy that uses data gathered from profiling to inform code improvements. In PGO, the profiling information is fed back into the development cycle to guide decisions on code restructuring, fine-tuning algorithms, or rewriting critical sections. This iterative process is valuable because it ensures that optimizations are based on actual performance metrics rather than on assumptions or theoretical models alone. For example, if profiling data indicates that a particular function is consistently a performance hotspot, developers might explore rewriting it in a more efficient language construct or use alternative algorithms that achieve the same functionality with lower computational overhead. The resulting improvements are then validated through further profiling, creating a cycle of continuous performance refinement.

Numerous tools have been developed to facilitate the profiling process across different programming environments. Common profiling tools include GNU gprof, Valgrind's Callgrind, and Visual Studio Profiler for desktop and enterprise applications. For Java environments, tools like JProfiler and VisualVM are popular choices, while Python developers often rely on cProfile and Py-Spy. These tools vary in their capabilities, with some providing detailed CPU and memory analytics, and others offering high-level overviews that are easier to interpret. The selection of an appropriate profiling tool depends on the specific needs of the application and the nature of the performance issues being investigated. In many cases, multiple tools are used in tandem to ensure that the profiling data is comprehensive and accurate.

When it comes to empirical testing, a systematic methodology is essential to obtaining reliable and meaningful performance data. The process begins with an experimental setup designed to simulate the expected operating environment of the application. This setup includes selecting appropriate input sizes, configuring system parameters, and ensuring that the testing conditions are controlled to minimize variability. Data collection follows, where performance metrics such as runtime and resource usage are recorded. This data is then subjected to statistical analysis to identify patterns and draw conclusions about the algorithm's behavior. Visualization techniques, such as plotting performance curves or creating histograms, are often employed to make the data easier to interpret. Such methods not only highlight the average performance but also illustrate how the algorithm performs under various stress conditions, including peak load scenarios.

Interpreting profiling results requires careful analysis. Raw data obtained from profiling tools must be scrutinized to distinguish between meaningful performance issues and noise that might result from environmental factors or measurement inaccuracies. Statistical techniques often come into play; for example, calculating averages, variances, and confidence intervals can help in making sense of the collected data. Visualization tools further enhance understanding, allowing developers to see trends over time and across different input sizes. Ultimately, the interpretation of profiling results is guided by the principles of data analysis: correlating the gathered metrics with known performance bottlenecks, establishing cause-and-effect relationships, and identifying areas where optimization would yield the greatest improvements.

Despite the effectiveness of profiling and benchmarking, there are common pitfalls that developers must watch out for. One frequent mistake is the inconsistency of testing environments. Differences in hardware, background processes, and even changes in system load can lead to variations in performance measurements, thus compromising the repeatability and accuracy of the benchmarks. Another common issue is misinterpreting data—for example, drawing conclusions from short-term fluctuations without considering long-term trends or failing to account for overhead introduced by the profiling tools themselves. To avoid these pitfalls, it is important to standardize the testing environment as much as possible and to use automated, repeatable testing procedures that minimize the influence of extraneous factors.

The techniques for analyzing profiling data stress the need for a methodical approach where each step—from data collection through statistical analysis to interpretation—is performed carefully and systematically. Whether using CPU, memory, or I/O profiling, the overarching goal is to obtain a data-driven understanding of where the algorithm's performance can be improved. This understanding then feeds back into the optimization cycle, where targeted changes are implemented, profiled, and re-evaluated to ensure that performance improvements are sustained under real-world conditions.

Overall, the integration of profiling and empirical methods into the performance evaluation process is indispensable. These methods bridge the gap between theoretical analysis and practical application by providing concrete, actionable insights derived from real-world testing.

Profiling helps identify specific areas of the code that require optimization, while benchmarking serves as a tool to measure progress against established performance criteria. By adhering to rigorous empirical methodologies and utilizing robust data analysis techniques, developers can ensure that their algorithms not only meet theoretical performance goals but also excel under actual operating conditions.

Profiling and empirical testing form the backbone of performance validation in algorithm optimization. They provide the necessary evidence to justify optimization efforts, guide code improvements, and ultimately contribute to the creation of high-performance software. Through careful experimental design, systematic data collection, and thorough analysis, these methods empower developers to address performance issues efficiently and effectively. The continuous cycle of measuring, analyzing, and optimizing ensures that software remains robust, scalable, and capable of meeting the increasingly demanding requirements of modern applications.

7.5 Algorithm Visualization Tools

Algorithm visualization is the process of using graphical representations to illustrate how algorithms execute and process data. This approach converts abstract code and theoretical concepts into visual forms, making it easier for developers, students, and practitioners to understand the flow of execution and the manipulation of data. Visualization helps transform complex procedures into accessible visual narratives, allowing one to observe the dynamic behavior of algorithms in action, from the initiation of inputs to final outputs.

One of the primary benefits of using visualization tools is that they deepen understanding of algorithm behavior. By providing a graphical window into the seemingly black-box operations of an algorithm, these tools simplify the debugging process and help identify logical errors. Visualization makes the intricate operations of algorithms transparent, a vital feature in both educational settings and professional development. It also serves to enhance algorithm teaching, as students can see real-time progression, which reinforces classroom theoretical explanations with hands-on demonstration of each step.

There are various types of visualization techniques that cater to different aspects of algorithm behavior. Flowcharts, for example, provide a high-level view of the algorithm's control structures, displaying decision points, loops, and the sequence of operations in a clear, hierarchical diagram. Step-by-step animations take this further by demonstrating each individual step of the algorithm as it processes data, often highlighting lines of code or specific operations in real time. Graphs are used to show data relations, such as comparing the performance of different parts of an algorithm or representing the structure of underlying data. Interactive visualizations allow users to engage with the model by changing input parameters or pausing and resuming execution, thereby providing a dynamic exploration of how algorithms handle variations in data and conditions.

Visualization tools are also specifically designed to help in visualizing data structures, an important aspect of understanding algorithm implementation. Specialized environments can depict arrays, linked lists, trees, and graphs with clear layouts and annotations that describe each element's position and relationship to others. For instance, arrays can be shown as linear sequences, while trees are commonly represented as hierarchical structures with nodes and branches that elegantly illustrate parent-child relationships. Graphs, on the other hand, can be visualized using nodes and edges that show both the connectivity and the weight of connections. This immediate visual feedback aids in grasping the organization and functionality of the data structures that are integral to efficient algorithm design.

A number of common visualization tools have been developed to support this need for clarity. VisuAlgo, for instance, is a powerful tool that provides interactive visualizations for a wide range of algorithms, including sorting, searching, and graph algorithms. AlgoViz is another platform that offers similar functionalities across various algorithm categories, and Python Tutor gives beginners an accessible way to visualize code execution, presenting the state of variables and control flow at each step of a program. These tools are widely used in both academic and development environments due to their ease of use and the clarity they bring to complex algorithmic concepts.

Among these tools, VisuAlgo stands out for its comprehensive features and interactive animations. VisuAlgo covers a broad set of algorithms ranging from basic sorting and searching techniques to complex graph algorithms and dynamic programming. Its user interface is designed to be intuitive, allowing users to select specific algorithms and observe their execution over time. The tool carefully highlights the operations performed at each step, such as comparisons, swaps, or recursive calls, and displays the data structure transformations as the algorithm progresses. This interactive experience not only demystifies how algorithms work but also provides learners with a hands-on approach to understanding why particular algorithms perform differently under varying conditions.

Python Tutor, known colloquially as pytut, offers a step-by-step visualization of code execution, which is particularly useful for beginners learning the fundamentals of programming. Unlike tools that focus solely on algorithms, Python Tutor dissects each line of code and displays the state of the program's memory, including variables and data structures. This granular level of detail helps novices visualize what happens when a function is called, how loops iterate over data, and where values are stored and modified. The clarity afforded by Python Tutor can be instrumental in bridging the conceptual gap between code writing and execution, thereby enhancing both learning and debugging.

Graph algorithms often require specialized tools that can capture the complexity of networks and relationships. Grapher tools such as Graphviz and Gephi are designed to visualize structures like graphs and networks with great precision. Graphviz uses the DOT language to describe graphs in a manner that emphasizes node relationships and connectivity through various layout algorithms, while Gephi offers an interactive environment where users can manipulate graph properties dynamically and observe changes in real time. These tools are particularly useful for understanding algorithms that perform traversals, shortest path computations, or flow optimizations in networked data. By providing a clear depiction of nodes and edges, these applications simplify the study of interconnected data patterns and contribute significantly to both theoretical understanding and practical debugging.

The benefits of algorithm visualizations are manifold. Visual representations can transform abstract, mathematical descriptions into concrete images that are easier to comprehend. This conversion is crucial for learners who might otherwise struggle with the symbolic representations of algorithm theory. Beyond improving comprehension, visual tools enhance user engagement and retention, as the visual formats provide a cognitive anchor that links theory with practice. For educators, visualizations serve as a pedagogical aid that reinforces lecture material, making it easier for students to grasp challenging concepts and retain them over time. Additionally, these tools allow developers to fine-tune implementations by visually comparing expected flows with actual performance, thereby supporting more accurate and effective debugging and optimization.

Another key advantage of visualization tools is the use of animations to reinforce learning. Animated representations of algorithm execution show the progression of the algorithm over time, highlighting transitions between states and the incremental changes in data structures. These animations are particularly effective in demonstrating recursive processes, where the call stack and variable states change dynamically with each recursion. Animation also plays a critical role in illustrating parallel execution, where multiple threads or processes interact concurrently. By making the abstract dynamics of concurrent operations visible, animations help in understanding the interplay between competing processes and the potential for issues like race conditions or deadlocks.

Despite their many benefits, visualization tools also face certain challenges. One common issue is the oversimplification of complex algorithms. To make visualizations accessible, some tools may abstract away critical details, which can lead to a superficial understanding of the underlying processes. While simplicity aids comprehension, the loss of nuance may prevent users from appreciating the full complexity of certain algorithms, particularly those with non-trivial optimizations or hidden performance trade-offs. Technical issues also arise with visualization tools, such as difficulties in handling very large data sets or ensuring that animations remain responsive under heavy computational loads. Furthermore, the need to balance clarity with detail means that not all aspects of algorithm execution can be captured comprehensively in a single visualization, leading to potential gaps in understanding if used in isolation.

In overcoming these challenges, it is important for users of visualization tools to complement them with traditional code analysis and documentation. While visualizations provide immediate insights, they should be integrated with deeper theoretical study and practical experimentation to achieve a well-rounded understanding. Educators and developers are encouraged to use multiple visualization tools where possible, cross-referencing their outputs to obtain a more holistic view of algorithm behavior. Moreover, continuous feedback and updates from the community play an essential role in refining these tools, ensuring that they evolve along with technological advancements and user needs.

Ultimately, the incorporation of visualization tools into the study and implementation of algorithms significantly enhances both learning and development processes. These tools serve as a bridge between the abstract world of algorithm theory and the tangible world of software execution. They provide an intuitive way to see how data flows through an algorithm, how structures are modified, and where potential inefficiencies might lie. Through interactive interfaces, detailed animations, and clear graphical representations, algorithm visualization tools empower users to understand and improve algorithms more effectively.

The integration of these visual aids into everyday programming and education not only demystifies complex processes but also promotes an iterative approach to problem solving, where continuous observation and feedback lead to incremental improvements. By transforming theoretical concepts into accessible visual formats, such tools pave the way for enhanced collaboration among students, educators, and professionals. They foster an environment where insights gleaned through visualization can directly inform code improvements and algorithmic innovations, ultimately resulting in software that is both robust and optimized for performance.

Algorithm visualization tools are indispensable in modern software development and algorithm education. These tools, ranging from simple flowcharts to elaborate dynamic animations, provide clarity, improve engagement, and act as effective debugging aids. They help visualize critical data structures, elucidate the flow of execution, and offer a practical means of verifying theoretical analysis through real-world simulation. While challenges remain, particularly with balancing detail and clarity, continued advancements in visualization technology are poised to address these issues, further solidifying the role of visualizations in the study and application of algorithms.

8

Practical Applications and Exercises

This chapter focuses on the application of algorithms and data structures in real-world scenarios to reinforce learning and understanding. It offers hands-on exercises that encourage readers to implement various algorithms, enhancing their coding skills and problem-solving abilities. The chapter also presents real-world case studies that showcase how algorithms have solved practical problems across different industries, such as logistics, finance, and healthcare. Additionally, it suggests project ideas that allow readers to integrate their knowledge into creating functional applications. Finally, it emphasizes the importance of participating in development communities to foster learning, collaboration, and ethical considerations in algorithm use.

8.1 Hands-on Exercises

Hands-on exercises are designed as practical, interactive tasks that allow readers to internalize theoretical concepts by implementing algorithms and data structures directly in code. These exercises are structured to bridge the gap between abstract algorithmic theories and real-world programming applications. By engaging with carefully designed exercises, readers are provided with opportunities to enhance their coding proficiency while simultaneously reinforcing the key ideas learned from earlier chapters.

Regular practice is a cornerstone of developing strong problem-solving skills. Engaging in hands-on exercises not only cements theoretical knowledge but also builds the intuition required to approach unseen challenges effectively. When readers actively code solutions to algorithmic puzzles or data structure problems, they develop an understanding that goes beyond rote memorization of concepts. This active engagement is essential to cultivate critical thinking and to gain the confidence needed to tackle increasingly complex problems. As coding proficiency grows, the execution speed of writing and debugging code naturally improves, laying a solid foundation for tackling advanced topics in algorithm design and analysis.

One of the primary exercises in this section is the implementation of various sorting algorithms. Readers are encouraged to write code for classic methods such as bubble sort, quick sort, and merge sort, testing each algorithm on data sets of different sizes and characteristics. This exercise provides a practical understanding of the strengths and weaknesses of each approach. In particular, learners can compare the efficiency and execution times of these algorithms under varying conditions. The following sample code demonstrates a basic bubble sort implementation:

```
#include <stdio.h>

void bubbleSort(int arr[], int n) {
    int i, j, temp;
    for (i = 0; i < n-1; i++) {
        for (j = 0; j < n-i-1; j++) {
            if (arr[j] > arr[j+1]) {
                // Swap elements
                temp = arr[j];
                arr[j] = arr[j+1];
                arr[j+1] = temp;
            }
        }
    }
}

int main() {
    int data[] = {64, 34, 25, 12, 22, 11, 90};
    int n = sizeof(data)/sizeof(data[0]);
    bubbleSort(data, n);
    for (int i = 0; i < n; i++) {
        printf("%d ", data[i]);
    }
    return 0;
}
```

After compiling and executing the code, readers should observe the sorted output in the terminal, which confirms the correctness of the algorithm. Comparing such outputs and the time taken for sorting helps in understanding algorithm efficiency under different scenarios. This exercise not only reinforces the understanding of sorting techniques but also paves the way for exploring more complex algorithms.

Another essential exercise involves graph traversal using both Depth-First Search (DFS) and Breadth-First Search (BFS). Graph traversal techniques serve as a critical tool in many computational problems, including pathfinding, network analysis, and even scheduling tasks. In this exercise, learners are prompted to represent a simple graph and implement both DFS and BFS methods to traverse the nodes. The primary goal is to observe the order in which nodes are visited in each approach and to appreciate the differences in traversal strategies. Below is a pseudocode outline for DFS implemented in a depth-first manner:

```
// Pseudocode for Depth-First Search (DFS)
procedure DFS(node, visited):
    mark node as visited
    for each neighbor of node:
        if neighbor is not visited:
            DFS(neighbor, visited)
```

Similarly, readers should implement BFS, which uses a queue to ensure that nodes are visited level by level. By comparing the pseudocode for DFS and BFS, learners grasp both the conceptual and practical differences between the two. The tangible exercise of coding these traversals not only enhances understanding of algorithmic paradigms but also improves skills in managing data structures like stacks and queues.

Dynamic programming is another key area for hands-on exploration. In this challenge, readers will implement a dynamic programming solution, with tasks such as calculating the Fibonacci sequence using memoization or solving the Knapsack problem. For instance, implementing the Fibonacci sequence using memoization reduces redundant calculations by storing previously computed results. Below is an illustrative example in C:

```c
#include <stdio.h>

#define MAX 100

long long fib[MAX];

long long fibonacci(int n) {
```

```
    if(n <= 1)
        return n;
    if(fib[n] != -1)
        return fib[n];
    fib[n] = fibonacci(n-1) + fibonacci(n-2);
    return fib[n];
}

int main() {
    // Initialize memoization array with a sentinel value
    for (int i = 0; i < MAX; i++) {
        fib[i] = -1;
    }
    int n = 40; // Calculate the 40th Fibonacci number
    printf("Fibonacci(%d) = %lld\n", n, fibonacci(n));
    return 0;
}
```

This exercise provides a clear demonstration of how storing intermediate results can drastically improve the performance of recursive solutions. Such tasks encourage critical analysis of algorithm efficiency and highlight the practical benefits of dynamic programming.

Optimizing algorithms is a natural progression for learners who have already implemented basic versions of these solutions. In the optimization exercise, readers are provided with an existing algorithm and challenged to analyze its performance. The objective is to reduce the time complexity and improve memory usage by applying optimization techniques, such as eliminating unnecessary computations or utilizing better data structures. For example, if an algorithm has a quadratic time complexity, readers might investigate ways to reduce it to linear or logarithmic time. This exercise demands careful consideration of algorithmic design and the trade-offs involved, thereby fostering analytical skills that are indispensable in professional programming.

The exercises also extend to projects that simulate real-world applications. One suggested project is to develop a small application, such as a scheduling app or a simple game, that leverages multiple algorithms to serve a practical purpose. By integrating sorting, graph traversal, and dynamic programming into a single application, learners experience how these theoretical concepts can be used together to solve complex problems. Such projects not only solidify the understanding of individual algorithmic techniques but also teach valuable lessons in system architecture and interface design. Working on an application project provides a holistic view of how different components interact, which is fundamental for developing larger, production-quality systems.

Collaboration is another essential aspect of the hands-on learning process. Readers are strongly encouraged to share the code they write with peers for review. Receiving and providing code reviews is a practical way to identify areas of improvement and learn alternative techniques. Collaborative projects and peer reviews often expose participants to new perspectives and foster a community where knowledge is freely exchanged. This interaction is especially valuable in a field as dynamic as programming, where continuous learning and adaptation are key to staying current with industry trends.

Adding clear comments and documentation to code is a best practice that can never be overlooked. When writing code for these exercises, it is important to document the purpose of functions, explain algorithm choices, and clarify complex parts of the code through in-line comments. Good documentation ensures that others (and future versions of yourself) can understand and maintain the code effectively. For example, while implementing a sorting algorithm or a graph traversal, clear documentation facilitates easier debugging and further enhancements by collaborators. This habit not only supports collaborative work but also improves overall coding clarity.

In addition to these internal exercises, external coding challenges available on platforms such as LeetCode, HackerRank, and CodeSignal provide ample opportunities for readers to test and improve their skills. Participating in these challenges exposes learners to a wide variety of problems and encourages them to think critically under time constraints. Through these online platforms, readers can compare their solutions with those of others, thereby gaining insights into different approaches and optimization techniques. The experience of coding under challenge conditions is invaluable for improving algorithmic reasoning and speeding up problem-solving capabilities.

A critical part of the learning process is the reflection on the outcomes of these exercises. After completing a task or project, readers should take time to analyze their solutions, identify any shortcomings or errors, and understand the underlying reasons for these issues. Reflecting on what was successful and what could be improved helps solidify the learning experience. This reflection might involve writing a brief report on the exercise, summarizing the approach taken, the challenges encountered, and the strategies used to overcome those challenges. Through such reflective practice, insights are gained that foster continuous improvement in both technical skills and overall problem-solving strategies.

The exercises described in this section collectively reinforce the connection between theoretical knowledge and practical application. By implementing sorting algorithms, coding graph traversals, tackling dynamic programming challenges, and optimizing algorithm performance, readers gain a well-rounded experience that is essential for mastering the craft of programming. Each exercise builds upon previous lessons and encourages the application of multiple algorithms within larger, project-based contexts. The integrated practice provided

241

in these tasks fosters a deeper understanding of algorithmic principles and nurtures the problem-solving mindset required for both academic and professional success. Engaging with these practical exercises ultimately leads to the development of not only sound coding skills but also the analytical capabilities necessary for designing efficient and robust algorithms.

8.2 Real-World Case Studies

Real-world case studies serve as detailed analyses of actual problems where algorithms have been employed successfully to deliver concrete solutions. By examining these case studies, readers gain insight into the application of abstract theories under practical constraints. These studies provide a lens through which the transformative power of algorithms can be understood in contexts that span diverse industries, thereby deepening both technical knowledge and practical appreciation.

Studying real-world examples is fundamental in bridging the gap between academic concepts and practical implementation. It is through these detailed examinations that readers appreciate how theoretical principles, when implemented correctly, can address complex challenges. Industry case studies not only help in understanding the mechanics behind algorithm design but also highlight the critical factors that contribute to the success or failure of a solution. For beginners, such analyses allow them to observe the evolution of an idea from a conceptual framework into a working system, reinforcing the notion that algorithms have tangible, far-reaching impacts across various sectors.

One illuminating case study is that of online recommendation systems. Major companies in the digital marketplace, such as Netflix and Amazon, leverage personalized recommendation algorithms to enhance user experience. These systems analyze user behavior, browsing history, and past interactions to suggest content, products, or services tailored to individual preferences. The algorithms behind these recommendations rely on filtering techniques and machine learning models that continuously adapt to user feedback. The practical implementation of these systems has revolutionized the way consumers interact with digital platforms, emphasizing the role of data-driven decision-making in building effective recommendation engines.

Another compelling instance is the use of algorithms in route optimization within logistics. Transport and delivery companies face the challenge of minimizing transportation costs while ensuring timely delivery across extensive networks. Algorithms such as Dijkstra's algorithm and the A* search algorithm are employed to compute the shortest or most efficient paths between nodes in a route network. These algorithms evaluate multiple factors, including distance, traffic conditions, and load capacities, to determine the optimal route. As logistics companies integrate these optimization techniques into their operational workflow, they are able to achieve significant efficiency gains, reduce fuel consumption, and improve customer satisfaction. This case study underscores the practical importance of algorithmic solutions in managing resources and time—a critical consideration in the competitive field of logistics.

Social network analysis represents another domain where algorithms play a critical role. Social media platforms collect vast amounts of data on user interactions, such as friend connections, messages, and shared content. Graph algorithms process this data to uncover patterns, identify influential users, and generate recommendations for new connections. By modeling social networks as graphs with nodes and edges, platforms can deploy algorithms that measure centrality, detect clusters, and analyze community structures. These insights inform strategic decisions in marketing, content distribution, and user engagement, demonstrating the significance of algorithms in extracting actionable intelligence from seemingly unstructured social data.

Search engines provide an illustrative example of the complexity and sophistication of algorithmic design. The process of ranking web pages and retrieving relevant results in response to a query depends on intricate algorithms that account for a multitude of factors—ranging from keyword relevance and page authority to user interaction signals. Algorithms such as PageRank and numerous modern refinements evaluate the interconnectedness of web pages to prioritize content that best meets the user's informational needs. Through continuous iteration and improvement, search engines have evolved to deliver highly accurate and contextually relevant results. This case study elucidates how layered algorithmic strategies can handle enormous datasets while providing performance at scale, thereby reinforcing the crucial role of algorithms in information retrieval systems.

Healthcare is yet another domain where algorithms are making a significant impact. In medical settings, predictive analytics have become an invaluable tool in diagnosing diseases early and managing patient care efficiently. Algorithms are used to analyze large datasets of patient records, medical imaging, and genetic information. Predictive models can identify risk factors and suggest proactive measures to prevent the progression of diseases. For instance, machine learning algorithms have been developed to detect early signs of conditions such as cancer, diabetes, and heart disease, thereby enabling timely intervention. The practical application of these algorithms not only improves patient outcomes but also enhances the overall efficiency of healthcare systems. By examining this case study, readers understand that the implementation of algorithmic techniques is both a scientific and an ethical imperative in contexts where human lives are directly affected.

The financial sector also benefits greatly from the application of algorithms. In financial market analysis, algorithms are central to tasks such as implementing trading strategies, detecting fraudulent transactions, and assessing risk. Automated trading systems use complex algorithms to analyze market trends, execute trades at optimal times, and adjust strategies in response to real-time data. Fraud detection systems, on the other hand, employ anomaly detection techniques and pattern recognition algorithms to safeguard financial transactions. These applications highlight not only the efficiency but also the precision that algorithms contribute to the management of financial data. With the growing importance of data security and risk management, understanding these case studies provides crucial insights into how modern financial institutions maintain competitive advantage and regulatory compliance.

Game development is a field that vividly illustrates the creative and technical possibilities of algorithmic applications. In developing video games, algorithms are used for a wide range of tasks including pathfinding, artificial intelligence (AI), and procedural generation. Pathfinding algorithms enable non-player characters (NPCs) to navigate complex environments, making gameplay more immersive. AI algorithms govern the behavior of game entities, contributing to challenging and dynamic interactions that respond to player choices. Procedural generation algorithms automatically create game content, such as terrain and story elements, ensuring a unique

245

experience each time the game is played. This integration of different algorithmic approaches demonstrates how theoretical techniques can be cohesively applied to produce engaging and interactive entertainment platforms.

Across these varied case studies, several key lessons emerge. One common insight is the importance of tailoring algorithmic solutions to specific problem contexts. While core principles may remain consistent, the practical constraints and objectives of each application necessitate adaptations and optimizations in algorithm design. For instance, the demands of real-time processing in search engines differ significantly from the batch processing requirements in healthcare analytics. Another important observation is that successful implementations often involve integrating multiple algorithmic techniques. Whether it is combining collaborative filtering with content-based approaches in recommendation systems or leveraging both heuristic and exact methods in route optimization, the interplay of various algorithms is frequently essential for achieving optimal performance.

Additionally, these case studies reveal that experimenting with algorithmic parameters and settings can yield substantial improvements in efficiency and effectiveness. This iterative process of testing, evaluation, and refinement is intrinsic to the development of robust solutions. In many cases, the deployment environment—such as system hardware, data scale, and user expectations—plays a decisive role in determining the final algorithmic design. The continuous feedback loop between theory, simulation, and real-world testing cultivates a deeper understanding of the practical considerations that influence algorithm performance.

Looking to the future, emerging trends promise to further expand the applications of algorithms in real-world scenarios. Advances in computing hardware, the increasing availability of big data, and the continuous evolution of machine learning techniques are setting the stage for even more sophisticated algorithmic solutions. Areas such as autonomous transportation, smart city infrastructure, and personalized medicine are likely to witness significant innovation driven by next-generation algorithms. These advancements, while building upon established foundations, will necessitate a renewed focus on ethical considerations, transparency, and accountability in algorithm design. By exploring future prospects, learners are encouraged to think critically about how emerging technologies might shape the next wave of algorithm-driven innovations.

The detailed examination of these diverse case studies underscores the critical role that algorithms play across multiple sectors. Whether optimizing delivery routes in logistics, enhancing search engines, improving healthcare diagnostics, or crafting immersive gaming experiences, the practical application of algorithms is evident. These real-world scenarios not only validate theoretical constructs but also inspire ongoing innovation and adaptation in algorithm design. Through this exploration, readers gain a comprehensive view of how the fusion of theory and practice leads to solutions that are both efficient and transformative.

This exploration into real-world cases demonstrates that algorithms are not just mathematical abstractions but are powerful tools that drive progress in everyday applications. The insights gleaned from examining these varied scenarios encourage an adaptive mindset and a readiness to apply learned principles in dynamic environments. The integration of theory with hands-on experience, as illustrated through these case studies, reinforces the value of a multidisciplinary approach to problem-solving. Observing the tangible benefits of these algorithmic applications fosters a deeper understanding of their potential and prepares learners to contribute meaningfully to future advancements in the field.

8.3 Project Ideas

Project ideas are designed as practical avenues for applying theoretical knowledge to create functional applications. These projects not only reinforce the concepts learned but also encourage experimentation with various algorithms and design paradigms, thereby deepening overall understanding of software development methodologies. By tackling small, manageable projects, readers are able to build confidence and develop a problem-solving mindset that is critical for advanced programming work.

One of the most accessible projects is the development of a simple calculator application. In this project, readers implement a basic tool that performs arithmetic operations such as addition, subtraction, multiplication, and division. This exercise reinforces fundamental algorithmic logic by requiring the integration of user input parsing, error handling, and the application of arithmetic operators. The design of such an application emphasizes the importance of clear logic and concise code organization, which are key elements in building reliable software. This project also invites further enhancements, such as adding support for more complex operations or integrating a graphical user interface, which can serve as stepping stones to more advanced topics.

Building upon this foundation, another project idea involves creating a to-do list manager. This project is particularly useful for integrating sorting and filtering algorithms. In designing a to-do list application, readers are tasked with organizing tasks based on attributes such as priority, deadline, or category. Implementing sorting algorithms to manage lists dynamically and filtering features to view tasks by specific criteria introduces concepts of algorithm efficiency and user-centric design. The to-do list project not only illustrates the practical application of data structures like arrays and lists but also highlights the importance of maintaining intuitive and accessible user interfaces. Such projects simulate real-world software problems that require the seamless integration of multiple algorithmic principles.

Expanding into more creative territory, readers can develop a text-based adventure game. This project involves the use of decision trees and pathfinding algorithms, which are critical in constructing interactive narratives. In a text-based game, each decision point and narrative branch is represented through algorithmic logic that determines the subsequent storyline. Implementing decision trees helps in understanding conditional structures, while pathfinding algorithms introduce spatial reasoning, even in a textual setting. This project encourages learners to think creatively about how algorithms can control narrative flow and game outcomes. The text-based adventure serves as a robust framework for exploring game logic and narrative design while solidifying foundational programming constructs.

Another engaging project is building a web scraper for data collection. In this exercise, readers design an application that navigates web pages, extracts relevant data, and processes it using appropriate algorithms. Web scraping involves understanding of HTML parsing, regular expressions, and efficient data extraction techniques. By integrating these elements, learners are exposed to the challenges of data cleaning, processing, and storage. This project not only highlights the practical importance of algorithmic efficiency when dealing with large amounts of data but also emphasizes real-world applications in areas such as market research and data analysis. The experience of building a web scraper provides valuable insights into handling external data sources and responding to dynamic web content.

For a more visually oriented project, developing an interactive graph visualizer offers an excellent opportunity to combine data input and graphical representation using graph algorithms. This project prompts readers to create a tool where users input data, and the program then visualizes relationships and connections in the form of a graph. Through this task, learners explore data structures associated with graphs, such as nodes and edges, and apply algorithms that highlight connectivity and clustering. The resulting visualization tool not only demonstrates the practical application of graph theory but also sharpens skills in handling user interaction and dynamic data displays. This project exemplifies how algorithms can be used to create powerful visual representations of abstract data, making complex relationships more accessible.

In a similar vein, another compelling project is the development of a sorting algorithm comparer. Readers are encouraged to design an application that implements and benchmarks various sorting algorithms on diverse datasets. By measuring performance metrics such as execution time and memory usage, this project deepens the understanding of algorithm efficiency, highlights the nuances of different sorting methods, and illustrates the impact of dataset characteristics on performance. Such an application requires careful thought around both algorithm selection and the design of performance testing modules. The sorting algorithm comparer serves as a practical tool for visualizing theoretical concepts and offers a concrete demonstration of how different approaches yield varying outcomes in similar problem spaces.

A project that brings attention to the interdisciplinary nature of algorithm implementation is the social network analysis tool. This project involves building a tool that models social networks and applies connectivity algorithms to analyze relationships among users. By using graph-based representations, learners can implement algorithms that identify clusters, measure centrality, and detect communities within the network. This project highlights the real-world significance of graph algorithms while showcasing the application of network theory in contemporary digital platforms. Such a tool not only reinforces algorithmic principles but also fosters an awareness of the broader social implications and potential applications of these techniques in areas such as marketing, trend analysis, and information dissemination.

Addressing practical financial concerns, a personal finance tracker project offers an excellent platform for integrating data processing and algorithmic decision-making. Readers are tasked with creating a tool that tracks income, expenses, and budgeting data. Algorithms come into play for automating categorization, detecting spending patterns, and providing budgeting suggestions based on historical data. Developing a personal finance tracker involves not only the application of basic arithmetic and sorting algorithms but also touches upon statistics and simple predictive models. This project is particularly beneficial for illustrating how everyday problems can be addressed using algorithmic solutions and emphasizes the importance of practical applications in personal financial management.

For those interested in the rapidly expanding field of artificial intelligence, a machine learning predictor project introduces learners to the basics of predictive modeling. In this project, readers build a simple machine learning model that utilizes historical data to forecast outcomes. Through data preprocessing, algorithm selection, and iterative testing, learners explore fundamental concepts in machine learning such as regression, classification, and model evaluation. Although the project remains intentionally basic, it lays the groundwork for understanding more complex models and techniques. The machine learning predictor project is a compelling example of how algorithmic thinking translates into predictive analytics, providing a glimpse into the future of data-driven decision-making.

Finally, residents of technology-driven portfolios can benefit from the challenge of creating a portfolio website. This project not only serves as a showcase of personal projects and achievements but also integrates algorithms for dynamic content sorting and filtering. A portfolio website built by the reader can be enhanced with features that automatically update content based on the latest projects, enable search functionalities across shared work, and optimize user experiences through adaptive layouts. The integration of algorithmic elements such as sorting and filtering within the website design elevates the project from a simple static page to an interactive, data-driven application. Through this project, learners experience firsthand how backend algorithmic processes can enhance front-end user engagement and streamline content management.

The array of project ideas presented encourages a hands-on approach to learning that extends beyond theoretical considerations. Each project is carefully designed to highlight specific programming constructs and algorithmic strategies, while simultaneously offering practical applications that mirror everyday challenges. By engaging with these projects, readers not only solidify their understanding of the concepts but also gain practical experience in problem-solving, code organization, and the iterative process of software development.

As learners work on these projects, it is important to document the design decisions, challenges encountered, and strategies implemented throughout the development process. Such reflective practice aids in consolidating learning outcomes and prepares individuals for collaboration in professional settings, where peer review and code optimization are integral components. Furthermore, the iterative nature of these projects allows for continual improvement, encouraging readers to refine and enhance their applications over time.

Project-based learning creates an environment where theoretical knowledge is validated against real-world scenarios. The incremental complexity of the projects—from a simple calculator to an interactive portfolio website—guides learners through a progressive journey, ensuring that each concept is thoroughly understood before advancing to more challenging tasks. This comprehensive approach not only builds a solid foundation in both algorithms and programming but also nurtures an adaptive and innovative mindset, which is crucial for tackling future technological challenges.

The diversity of project ideas presented in this section underlines the versatility and practical relevance of algorithmic concepts. By integrating these projects into the learning process, readers are equipped with the skills to design, implement, and improve solutions that have direct applications in everyday computing tasks. The projects serve as tangible demonstrations of how algorithms translate into functional systems, thereby reinforcing the transformative potential of applied knowledge in computer science.

8.4 Collaboration and Community

Collaboration and community involvement are essential components in the growth of any programmer, providing avenues for continuous learning and professional development. Working alongside peers and contributing to shared projects enables individuals to exchange ideas, gain exposure to diverse problem-solving approaches, and enhance their technical skills beyond what solo study can offer. Establishing a connection with a community of developers not only enriches one's professional knowledge but also instills a culture of lifelong learning.

When individuals work in collaborative environments, the benefits become apparent in multiple dimensions. Sharing knowledge with peers allows new techniques and insights to be discovered and refined collaboratively. Such interactions often lead to improved coding practices as developers learn from each other's experiences, assess various methods, and apply lessons learned across different projects. Exposure to a multitude of perspectives helps identify unique solutions to challenging problems and encourages innovation that might not have been possible in isolation. The process of working on joint projects builds both technical competence and soft skills, such as communication and teamwork, which are invaluable in professional settings.

Online communities play a pivotal role in fostering these collaborative opportunities. Platforms such as GitHub, Stack Overflow, and other specialized coding forums offer spaces where developers can seek advice, share code, and contribute to larger repositories. Engaging with these communities provides access to a vast pool of shared knowledge and real-life solutions that are applicable to common and uncommon challenges alike. Participating in these platforms helps build a professional network and exposes individuals to the evolving best practices in the field, advancing both their technical expertise and their understanding of emerging trends.

Contribution to open source projects represents one of the most practical methods for honing coding skills. By participating actively in open source projects, individuals have the opportunity to engage directly with complex codebases and contribute improvements, bug fixes, or new features. Such contributions not only add value to the community but also serve as a demonstration of one's skills to potential employers and collaborators. The open source ecosystem encourages transparency and continuous learning while offering a real-world testing ground for designing, debugging, and optimizing algorithms. This exposure sharpens coding habits and reinforces the principles of quality software development, including modular design, version control, and documentation.

Choosing the right project to contribute to is a critical component of effective community participation. It is advisable for individuals to seek projects that align with their interests and technical proficiency, ensuring that contributions are both meaningful and engaging. Projects that resonate with personal passion often provide the motivation needed to overcome the initial challenges of joining established communities. Moreover, starting with smaller, well-documented repositories can build confidence and provide a foundation from which one can later progress to more complex endeavors. This strategic approach allows learners to set measurable goals while gradually increasing the scope and impact of their contributions.

Networking opportunities within collaborative communities can lead to substantial career advancements. Engaging with peers on online platforms or local meetups often results in connections that bridge the gap between academic learning and professional practice. These inter-actions can lead to referrals, mentorship arrangements, and invitations to participate in specialized projects or workshops. By investing time in community engagement, developers create personal branding that speaks to their reliability, expertise, and willingness to contribute to collective success. Such recognition often opens doors to job opportunities and collaborations that may otherwise remain inaccessible.

The landscape of collaboration today is supported by various effective tools designed to facilitate seamless project management and communication. Tools like Slack, Trello, and Git are integral in managing collaborative efforts in real time. Slack provides instantaneous communication channels that facilitate troubleshooting, idea exchange, and project updates. Trello offers a visual way to organize tasks and manage project milestones, enabling teams to monitor progress efficiently. Git, as a version control system, plays a crucial role in maintaining the integrity of codebases while allowing multiple collaborators to work on different aspects of a project simultaneously. Familiarity with these tools ensures that developers can participate actively in collaborative environments, streamline their contributions, and maintain high standards of code quality.

Active participation in discussions and forums is another important aspect of community engagement. Contributing to question-and-answer sessions on platforms such as Stack Overflow not only assists others in solving their technical problems but also deepens one's understanding by articulating solutions clearly. Engaging in these dialogues fosters a culture of mutual assistance where both asking questions and providing answers are valued. Frequent participation in discussion threads also creates the opportunity for continuous learning, as developers encounter varying approaches to similar problems and can compare their effectiveness.

An integral part of collaboration is the process of giving and receiving constructive feedback. Constructive criticism is vital for personal and professional growth as it highlights not only the strengths of a solution but also areas where improvements can be made. Receiving feedback from more experienced peers can accelerate learning by identifying subtle bugs or design oversights, while offering feedback to others reinforces one's own understanding of the subject matter. The exchange of constructive feedback fuels a healthy development environment, where each iteration of code contributes incrementally to the quality of the final product.

Mentorship in collaborative settings further strengthens the community. In any active development environment, experienced programmers often take on the role of mentors, providing guidance and sharing their expertise with those newer to the field. The benefits of mentorship are twofold: mentors refine their own understanding by explaining complex concepts, while mentees gain invaluable insights that would be difficult to obtain through self-study. This reciprocal relationship enhances not only the technical skills of both parties but also builds a sense of community support and interdependence that is essential for long-term career growth.

The impact of collaboration and community involvement is frequently reflected in career advancement and personal branding. Engaging actively with communities allows developers to build a robust portfolio of contributions that can be showcased in professional settings. Personal branding in the tech domain goes beyond a resume or cover letter; it is demonstrated through active participation in online forums, contributions to widely recognized projects, and a consistent ability to solve challenging problems collaboratively. This visibility enhances job prospects and creates a competitive edge in a field that continuously values innovation, reliability, and collaborative spirit. The pathways created by these engagements can lead to research opportunities, higher-level positions, and roles that influence future technology standards.

The commitment to collaboration and community is a catalyst for both personal and professional development. The collective effort of shared knowledge, the encouragement found in supportive networks, and the continuous flow of ideas foster an environment where every programmer, regardless of experience level, can grow. Collaborative endeavors provide an opportunity to remain updated with industry trends, widely adopt best coding practices, and adapt to the dynamic nature of technology. The cumulative benefit of this culture is not only evident in improved coding skills and project management capabilities but also in the ability to mentor future generations of developers, thereby perpetuating a cycle of continuous improvement.

Ultimately, the integration of collaboration into daily programming practice proves indispensable. Learning from others, contributing to shared projects, and providing feedback creates a holistic development atmosphere that no individual can achieve in isolation. The synergy created by working with others enhances the developer's ability to creatively solve problems, adopt emerging technologies, and remain agile in a rapidly changing technological landscape. Through active involvement in both online and offline communities, developers prepare themselves to face the increasingly complex challenges of modern software development. This ongoing collaborative interaction forms the backbone of professional development and accelerates career growth by exposing individuals to a diverse set of experiences, technical insights, and opportunities for innovation.

By immersing oneself in collaborative environments, researchers, hobbyists, and professional developers alike benefit from the expansive ecosystem of shared knowledge and collective improvement. The role of technology is continually redefined by its community of contributors. As each developer contributes their unique expertise and learns from the collective wisdom, the overall quality and capability of technological solutions are elevated. Engaging in collaboration not only contributes to personal technical growth but also paints a broader picture of how modern software is developed in ensemble rather than isolation.

In the current landscape of computer science and software engineering, the value of community and teamwork cannot be overstated. The principles gained through collaboration—shared problem-solving, iterative improvement, and mutual support—are directly translatable to professional settings and real-world applications. Developers who actively participate in their communities are better prepared to tackle complex challenges, adapt to rapid changes in technology, and drive forward innovation. This vibrant network of sharing and learning is a cornerstone of continuous improvement in the modern tech industry, paving the way for breakthroughs that rely on the collective expertise of the entire community.

Recognizing the importance of these collaborative efforts, it is essential for every developer to invest in building and nurturing their professional network. Whether through online coding forums, open source contributions, local meetups, or global conferences, the act of engaging with a community fosters both technical excellence and a sense of belonging in the ever-evolving world of technology. Embracing collaboration as a lifelong practice eventually leads to a rich professional tapestry, where ideas are freely exchanged, success is celebrated collectively, and future challenges are approached with confidence derived from shared experience.

8.5 Ethical Considerations

Ethical considerations in algorithm design involve the critical assessment of the social and moral impacts of technology on society. As algorithms increasingly influence decision-making processes in domains ranging from finance and healthcare to social media and law enforcement, it is imperative that developers and decision-makers assess the broader consequences of their designs. This responsibility extends beyond ensuring that algorithms perform efficiently and accurately; it requires a rigorous examination of how algorithms shape human behavior, impact social structures, and potentially perpetuate inequalities.

A primary ethical concern in algorithm design is the potential for bias. Algorithms are often built on historical data and human-crafted rules, mechanisms that can embed the biases that exist in their source material. When these biases are not recognized and addressed, algorithms can inadvertently produce outcomes that are unfair or discriminatory. For example, predictive models used in recruitment or loan approvals may disadvantage certain demographic groups if the training data reflects historic prejudices. Recognizing and mitigating bias involves critically evaluating data sources and algorithms, and continuously validating the fairness of outputs. It is crucial to adopt fairness-enhancing practices, such as balanced data collection, fairness-aware machine learning techniques, and regular audits to ensure that the algorithm does not reinforce pre-existing stereotypes or inequities.

Transparency in algorithm design is closely tied to the issue of bias and involves making algorithmic processes open and understandable to both users and stakeholders. Transparent algorithms enable individuals to see how decisions are made, fostering trust and accountability. For instance, when a recommendation engine or a predictive policing system is deployed, users and affected communities should have access to information about the factors that influence decision-making. Transparent design practices may include publishing model documentation, explaining the rationale behind certain parameters, and providing clear descriptions of the data processing methods used. By promoting transparency, developers can create systems that are not only technically sound but also ethically responsible and open to external scrutiny.

The ethical challenges related to data privacy form another critical dimension of algorithmic design. Modern algorithms often depend on vast amounts of personal data to function effectively, but the collection, storage, and use of such data come with significant privacy concerns. The ethical implication here is that individuals have a right to control their personal information and understand how it is used. In practice, this means designing systems that adhere to privacy-by-design principles, ensuring that data is collected with informed consent and used in ways that are consistent with ethical guidelines. Encryption, anonymization, and secure data handling practices are all necessary measures to protect personal information and maintain public trust in algorithmic solutions.

Accountability for algorithmic decisions is essential, especially when these decisions have far-reaching consequences for human lives. When an algorithm influences aspects such as employment opportunities, lending decisions, or even legal outcomes, it is crucial that there be clear lines of responsibility. Accountability ensures that if errors occur

261

or if decisions lead to adverse outcomes, there is a way to determine who is responsible and how to address the issue. This might involve establishing regulatory frameworks or having internal review boards where the design, deployment, and outcomes of algorithms are continuously monitored. Such measures not only mitigate risks but also contribute to a culture of responsibility and ethical governance in technology.

The social impact of algorithms cannot be underestimated. Algorithms shape the way people interact with digital platforms, influence public opinion, and impact societal structures. For example, algorithms curating content on social media have the power to affect public discourse by emphasizing certain narratives over others, potentially leading to polarization or the spread of misinformation. Similarly, in the workplace, algorithms that track performance or manage human resources can significantly alter work environments and employee behavior. This influence necessitates a thoughtful approach to algorithm design, one that considers the long-term societal implications alongside immediate performance goals. Evaluating the broader social impact of technology is a continuous process, requiring engagement with sociologists, ethicists, and the public to ensure that the balance between innovation and societal well-being is maintained.

Developing ethical algorithms that promote fairness and inclusivity is a goal that should be at the heart of every technological initiative. Ethical algorithms are those designed not only to improve efficiency or profitability but also to ensure equitable outcomes for all users. This involves a commitment to developing algorithms that are free from bias, transparent in their operation, and accountable to the public. Fairness in this context means that algorithms should treat all individuals with equal respect and consideration, regardless of background or identity.

The process of ensuring fairness may involve incorporating techniques such as differential privacy, bias correction algorithms, and fairness-aware training methods. As developers pursue these approaches, they engage directly with the ethical dimensions of their work, integrating principles of justice and equity into the very fabric of technological advancement.

Regulatory and legal frameworks play a pivotal role in shaping the ethical landscape of algorithm design and deployment. With governments and regulatory bodies increasingly recognizing the profound influence of technology, new regulations are emerging to govern the ethical use of algorithms. These frameworks are intended to protect user rights, ensure accountability, and provide a clear set of guidelines for ethical technology practices. For instance, laws surrounding data protection, such as the General Data Protection Regulation (GDPR) in Europe, set strict standards for the collection and processing of personal data. In the context of algorithmic decision-making, similar regulations are beginning to take shape, demanding greater transparency, fairness, and accountability. Adhering to such frameworks is not only a legal necessity but also an ethical imperative that fosters trust between technology providers and users.

Real-world case studies of ethical dilemmas in algorithm deployment provide critical lessons and prompt necessary reflection among developers and policymakers alike. Across various industries, there have been instances where algorithmic systems have raised significant ethical concerns, ranging from discriminatory practices in automated hiring to inadvertent privacy violations in data-driven marketing. These case studies serve as cautionary tales that highlight the importance of proactive ethical evaluation before, during, and after the implementation of technological solutions. By analyzing these examples, practitioners gain insight into the complexities and potential pitfalls associated with algorithmic systems, enabling them to formulate more robust strategies for mitigating ethical risks. Reflecting on these dilemmas reinforces the need for continuous improvement, not only in technical aspects but also as part of a broader commitment to societal well-being.

Public awareness and education are equally essential components in the ethical deployment of algorithms. As technology becomes ever more pervasive, there is a growing need to educate the public about how algorithms work and the ethical implications associated with their use. Informed users are better equipped to demand transparency, understand their rights, and participate in dialogues about technological governance. Educational initiatives might include public seminars, online courses, and outreach programs designed to demystify algorithmic processes and explain their impact on everyday life. Such efforts empower consumers and citizens to engage more actively in discussions about technological progress and to advocate for more ethical practices. By raising public awareness, the technology sector fosters an environment where ethical considerations become an integral part of the developmental narrative, rather than an afterthought.

The amalgamation of these ethical considerations highlights the multidimensional nature of algorithm design. Developers must navigate a complex landscape that requires balancing efficiency with fairness, innovation with accountability, and autonomy with public interest. The consequences of neglecting ethical considerations are not merely technical; they reverberate through society, impacting lives, communities, and democratic processes. In recognizing this, the field moves toward more responsible poetics of technological development—where ethical integrity and technical excellence are seen not as opposing forces but as mutually reinforcing principles. Each decision in the design and deployment of algorithms carries with it an ethical weight that must be acknowledged and addressed through diligent, ongoing reflection and committed action.

Through the lens of ethical evaluation, developers are better prepared to chart a path forward that upholds the values of fairness, inclusivity, and transparency. These principles, when integrated into the design process, contribute to the creation of algorithmic systems that are both technically effective and socially responsible. As technology continues to reshape the fabric of society, maintaining an ethical perspective becomes increasingly crucial. Innovations in algorithmic methods must be accompanied by robust ethical practices that guide the transformation of abstract ideas into real-world technologies that enhance the human experience without compromising moral standards.

The challenges ahead are significant, but so are the opportunities for positive impact if ethical considerations remain at the forefront of technological advancement. Continuous dialogue among technologists, ethicists, regulators, and the public is essential for developing best practices that balance progress with principled action. The commitment to ethical principles in algorithm development is not only a professional responsibility but also a societal imperative—ensuring that as our capabilities expand, they do so in a way that respects and promotes the dignity, rights, and well-being of all people.

Incorporating these ethical principles into every stage of algorithm development creates a foundation for trust and accountability. It prepares the way for technological innovations that do not merely serve as tools for efficiency but also as vehicles for social progress. The journey toward more ethical technology is ongoing and requires persistent attention, thoughtful design, and an unwavering commitment to public good. By embracing a responsible and transparent approach in algorithm design, society is better positioned to harness the potential of technology while safeguarding against its inherent risks.

8.5. ETHICAL CONSIDERATIONS